Elegant Quilts, Country Charm

APPLIQUÉ DESIGNS IN COTTON AND WOOL

Leonie Bateman and Deirdre Bond-Abel

Martingale®
Create with Confidence

Dedications

To my beautiful family—Dan, Ellen, and Jess—whom I love with all my being. How can I ever thank you enough for your never-ending love, support, and encouragement in allowing me to follow my dream?

To Nanny and Gramps, for caring so much and being the best in-laws any girl could ever want. You both mean so much to me.

— *Leonie*

To my mother and father, for being the best parents in the world in every way. I love you so much.

To my sister, Jeanette, and brothers, Phillip and Tony, for sharing their lives with me.

To my beautiful children, Casey and Mitchell. Thank you for your love and support. I know you're as proud of me as I am of you. You are two beautiful, creative souls whom I cherish every day.

To my darling husband, Phil, for your love, support, encouragement, and understanding. Thank you for letting me follow my dreams.

— *Deirdre*

Acknowledgments

We'd like to thank:

Helen, for encouraging us to take our designs out into the marketplace. Her guidance, support, and friendship over the years have been invaluable.

"Big Al" (Alan Murphy) of XLN Fabrics, who has always stuck by us, encouraged us, and given us the confidence to keep pushing forward.

Peter and Lynne Wilson of Highland Quiltworks, for introducing us to wool so long ago and starting us on this journey.

Martingale, for giving us this opportunity, which for both of us was only a dream.

Elegant Quilts, Country Charm:
Appliqué Designs in Cotton and Wool

© 2012 by Leonie Bateman and Deirdre Bond-Abel

Martingale®
19021 120th Ave. NE, Suite 102
Bothell, WA 98011 USA
ShopMartingale.com

Printed in China
17 16 15 14 13 12   8 7 6 5 4 3 2 1

Library of Congress Cataloging-in-Publication Data is available upon request.

ISBN: 978-1-60468-076-8

Credits

President & CEO: Tom Wierzbicki

Editor in Chief: Mary V. Green

Design Director: Paula Schlosser

Managing Editor: Karen Costello Soltys

Technical Editor: Laurie Baker

Copy Editor: Marcy Heffernan

Production Manager: Regina Girard

Cover & Text Designer: Shelly Garrison

Illustrator: Laurel Strand

Photographer: Brent Kane

Special thanks to Lianne and Bryce Anderson of Arlington, Washington, for generously allowing us to photograph in their home.

Mission Statement

Dedicated to providing quality products and service to inspire creativity.

Contents

Introduction

We're Leonie and Deirdre, and we've been the owners of The Quilted Crow quilt shop since 2005. Our shop is housed in a beautiful old sandstone church built in 1865. It's located in historic Hobart, the capital city of Tasmania, Australia. We love to fill our shop with beautiful displays, including old bits of furniture to store the fabrics, quilts, and other needful treasures our customers love.

We've both been designing quilts for some time now, but over the last six years the main focus of our designs has been using felted wool in combination with reproduction fabrics. Our styles are quite similar, but we each design our own work separately. We both love antique quilts and take inspiration from them, mixing traditional styles and adding a new twist to them by using beautiful felted wool for the appliqué.

For Deirdre, my first love is traditional-style piecing and I use this as my starting point— followed by the appliqué.

For Leonie, my first love is appliqué, and I often use it as my starting point. I like to let the project grow and develop along the way.

Come join us on this journey, as together we share our love of working with two of our favorite fabrics—felted wool and reproduction cotton prints.

— Deirdre and Leonie

Appliquéing with Wool

If you've never appliquéd with wool before, you're in for a treat. Once wool's been felted, the edges won't fray, so you don't need to turn them under—and the fabric itself is quite flexible and forgiving, making it a real pleasure to use for appliqué.

In this section, we'll cover the techniques we use for preparing appliqués and positioning them on the background fabric, the tools and supplies we like, and our favorite stitches.

WHAT IS FELTED WOOL?

First, let's explain the differences between felted wool and wool felt. Felted wool is a *woven* wool fabric that's washed and agitated in hot water and dried with heat. This process condenses and compacts (felts) the fibers and results in a lovely soft and fluffy fabric that won't fray. Projects made with felted wool can be laundered without the worry of the pieces shrinking or fraying.

Wool felt, on the other hand, is made up of individual wool fibers that have been wet, heated, and tightly compressed together, as opposed to woven together. Wool felt cannot be laundered as successfully as felted wool.

CHOOSING WOOL FOR APPLIQUÉ

We only use felted wool made from 100% wool fibers. When choosing wool for appliqué, look for wool that isn't too thick, and choose a variety of colors and textures that will add some visual interest to your work.

Hand-dyed wools are great to have in your wool stash. Because they're hand dyed, there can be many subtle variations in color within a piece, which is a good thing—use the light and dark sections from a hand-dyed piece to create a flower or a leaf and see how different it can look than if you just use a solid color. Different patterns, such as plaid or herringbone, are great for adding visual texture to backgrounds, large leaves, or pots. And make sure you include some "uglies" (wool pieces in patterns and colors you might

not like on their own) in your stitched piece. Just as with cotton fabrics, the unexpected can sometimes add just the right touch to make a piece pop.

PREPARING WOOL FOR APPLIQUÉ

When we receive wool fabric in our shop, the first thing we do is take it home and put it through the felting process. Doing this ensures that the wool is ready to use for a project. We suggest that when you purchase wool you ask if it has already been felted. If it hasn't, then we recommend you launder it as soon as you get home, bearing in mind that it's going to shrink.

THREADS AND TOOLS FOR WOOL APPLIQUÉ

In addition to the tools and supplies you need for regular quilting, you'll need some threads and tools for doing wool appliqué. Below are some of our favorites:

- Stranded cotton embroidery floss. We prefer DMC and Madeira brands.

- Ginnie Thompson Flower Thread. Flower thread is equal to two strands of embroidery floss.

- Size 11 milliner's needles and/or size 8 appliqué needles for hand sewing

- 4" fine-point embroidery scissors. This size is ideal for cutting tiny shapes and for cutting out shapes for reverse appliqué.

- Water-soluble glue stick

- General office stapler. We use this to temporarily attach appliqués to the background fabric. A 12" office stapler is also good to have on hand because the extra length makes it much easier to reach into places that a standard-size stapler can't.

- Marking tools: white pencil or marker, water-soluble marker, lead pencil

- Freezer paper

- Light box

- Rotary-cutting equipment

MAKING A MASTER PATTERN

Several of the appliqué designs in this book can be positioned by simply eyeballing the flowers, leaves, or stems. Other designs require symmetry to achieve a balanced look. For example, you may want to have the same sweep of the vine on all four of a quilt's appliquéd borders. The best way to make sure each piece is the same is to make a master pattern. Simply trace the pattern for the desired project onto a piece of paper (copy paper is fine) using a lead pencil. You'll then be able to center your background fabric over the master pattern and use it as a guide for placing the appliqués.

Because several of the patterns are too large to fit on one sheet of paper, you'll need to trace each individual section onto its own piece of paper, and then join the sections where indicated to make a complete pattern. Be sure to transfer the reference lines to the master pattern.

PREPARING THE BACKGROUND FOR APPLIQUÉ

There are a number of ways to prepare your background fabric for appliqué. The method we describe here works well for both of us; however, if you have another method and are comfortable using it, continue to do so.

We prefer to align things precisely, so we mark reference lines on the background fabric to help us consistently align the appliqué pieces. To do this, we simply fold the background fabric in half vertically and horizontally or diagonally in both directions, depending on the design, and finger-press the folds. Often we mark over the fold lines with a water-soluble marker or white pencil or marker (for dark fabrics) so the lines are easier to see.

Some people prefer to place their appliqué pieces by eye and not use any reference lines. This method works well too. After all, if we look at a flowering plant in the garden, it grows in all different directions. The same can be said for appliqué—it doesn't have to be exact.

MAKING THE APPLIQUÉS

We both use freezer paper to make templates for cutting the appliqué shapes. The beauty of freezer paper is that you can reuse the templates a number of times before they no longer adhere to the wool and need to be replaced. Start by tracing one of each shape and make more as needed.

Storing Patterns

If you plan on reusing your templates, store them in small resealable plastic bags and label them accordingly for future use.

1. Trace each shape onto the dull side of a piece of freezer paper, leaving approximately ¼" to ½" between the shapes. Using paper scissors, roughly cut out each shape. With the shiny side down, iron each shape onto the right side of the selected piece of wool using a dry iron. Try not to press too hard on the wool so that you don't flatten the fabric too much.

2. Carefully cut out each piece along the drawn line and remove the freezer paper. Your shapes are now ready for placement onto your background piece.

Get the Most from Your Wool

Save every little scrap of wool—you'll be surprised what you can make with the leftovers. Tiny pieces are great for berries and leaves, while narrow pieces are perfect for stems.

APPLIQUÉING WOOL TO THE BACKGROUND

Once all the shapes are cut out, it's time to position and attach them to the background. The following is our favorite method for temporarily holding the appliqués

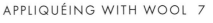

in place until they've been stitched. Some people are shocked when we tell them we use a water-soluble glue stick and an office stapler, but it works! Neither of us likes to use any sort of fusible web to attach our pieces, so the glue-and-stapler method is a great alternative for us. The staples are easy to remove with your fingers and because the wool is self-healing, they don't leave any marks on the appliqués.

1. Place the master pattern on a light box. Position the background fabric right side up over the pattern, aligning all reference points.

Preassembling Units

For appliqués that are made up of more than one piece, such as the center flower in "For Ellen" (page 32), stitch the pieces together, and then stitch the assembled unit to the background piece. It's easier to stitch one assembled unit to the background than to stitch each piece individually to the background.

2. Apply a dab of glue to the wrong side of each appliqué shape or preassembled unit. Follow the master pattern to gently press the shapes into place on the background, working from the bottom layer up. You can also use a glue stick along the length of stems and vines—gently run the glue along the strip, and then press a nice smooth curve into the wool following the outline on your pattern.

3. Once all of the pieces are in place, use your stapler and staple them for a firm hold. We've found if we just rely on the glue it isn't enough to keep the pieces in place when we're handling the project during the appliqué process. Give stapling a try—you'll be surprised at the result!

4. Refer to "Stitch Guide" at right and use a blanket stitch to appliqué the pieces in place using matching thread and your needle of choice. Remove the staples.

STITCH GUIDE

All of the appliqués are secured using a blanket stitch and embroidery floss or flower thread. Leonie uses one strand of DMC embroidery floss for all of her appliqué. When she wants more definition, such as in "Out on a Limb" (page 25), she uses two strands of floss. She uses a size 11 milliner's needle for all of her appliqué.

Deirdre uses one strand of Madeira embroidery floss or Ginnie Thompson Flower Thread, which is a single-strand cotton that is the equivalent thickness of two strands of embroidery floss, for her appliqué. She uses a size 8 appliqué needle, but we suggest you experiment with different threads and needles and use what works best for you.

When blanket-stitching pieces to the background, don't pull the thread up too tight, or the edges of the wool will curl up. Just let your thread rest on top of the appliqué. When we're blanket-stitching through multiple layers, we find that a stab stitch keeps our work nice and flat.

Occasionally some of our projects have a few additional embroidery elements that require the use of other stitches. Shown below are stitches that we commonly use.

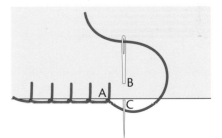

Blanket stitch

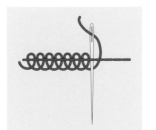

Pekinese stitch

Satin stitch

APPLIQUÉING A DOGTOOTH OR SCALLOPED BORDER

Don't be intimidated by the dogtooth or scalloped borders used in some of the designs. These borders are relatively easy to make; they just take a little time and patience. Like anything, after you've done it once, it will become much easier! The main thing is to be very careful when cutting out the pieces.

Cutting the Border Strips

1. Trace the side border for the selected design onto the dull side of a piece of freezer paper, repeating the design to extend the pattern to the length given. The borders will be cut longer than needed. Ensure that the piece of wool you're using for the dogtooth border has straight edges.

2. With the shiny side down, line up the straight edge of the freezer-paper pattern with the edge of the wool and iron the pattern in place.

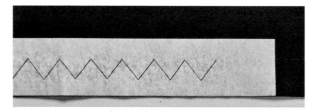

Line up the edge of the wool with the freezer-paper straight edge.

3. Very carefully cut out the border pattern using a pair of scissors with sharp points. Take care when cutting dogtooth borders so that you can use the leftover piece (shown at the top in the photo below) for the opposite side border. Remove the freezer paper from the border piece only.

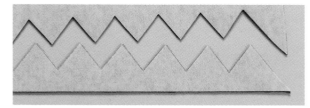

The border piece is on the bottom; the leftover piece at the top will be used for the opposite dogtooth border.

4. For the dogtooth border, to cut the remaining side border, lay the leftover piece from step 3 on your rotary mat. Align the ½" line of your rotary ruler along the inner points of the piece; cut along the straight edge of the ruler. For the scalloped border, repeat steps 1–3 to cut the remaining side border.

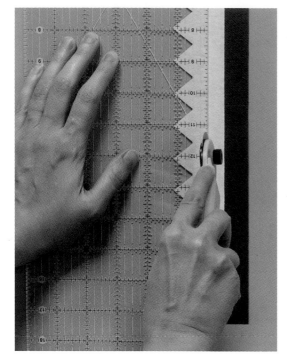

Cut ½" from the inner points of the leftover dogtooth-border piece to make the opposite side border.

5. Repeat steps 1–4 to make the top and bottom borders using the width given in the pattern instructions.

Positioning the Border Strips

1. Mark a reference line around the edge of the background fabric, as described in the project instructions. These lines will form a frame and act as a guide to place the border strips.

2. Fold the background fabric in half vertically and horizontally and finger-press the folds.

3. Place a border strip on the appropriate edge of the background. Center the top point of a dogtooth border or the center of an outer curve of a scalloped border on the center fold line of the background fabric. The *inner* points of the border

strip need to sit right on top of the drawn reference line. You'll have excess at one or both ends, which will be trimmed away later.

Align the center top point of the border with the center fold line of the background fabric. Position the inner points on the drawn line.

4. Repeat steps 1–3 for the remaining sides of the quilt. It doesn't matter in which order you place them. Make sure there are no openings in the "frame." The ends that overlap at the corners will be trimmed after the border is appliquéd in place. Once you're happy with the placement, hold the strips in place with a dab of fabric glue and some staples.

5. Appliqué the decorative edge of each border strip. Trim the excess so the edges just overlap each other. Remove the staples.

REVERSE APPLIQUÉ

Many of our designs feature reverse appliqué, which simply means that we cut out a section of the main appliqué and slip another fabric between the background fabric and the appliqué so that a second color shows through. By incorporating these cutout areas, we're able to easily add extra color and dimension to a design. In some designs you'll find we placed wool behind wool, which gives a three-dimensional look; for other designs we used cotton behind the wool. Either way, reverse appliqué provides a look that's visually pleasing.

1. Refer to "Making the Appliqués" (page 6) to make the main shape from wool. Cut away the areas indicated using your embroidery scissors.

2. Cut a piece of wool or cotton that's larger than the main shape and place it under the main shape so that the right side is visible through the cutout areas. Use a couple dabs of glue and some staples to hold it in place.

Place the wool appliqué shape with the cutouts onto a larger piece of wool or cotton fabric.

3. Blanket-stitch around the inside edges of the cutout areas to attach the two pieces.

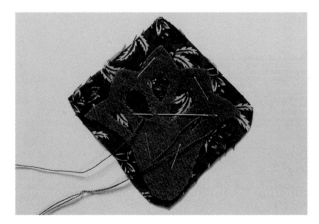

4. Trim the larger piece so there isn't any fabric showing around the main shape.

CHAIN PIECING

Chain piecing can be used when you're making multiples of the same unit. This method saves time and thread. It's also beneficial to chain piece because most sewing machines will take up fabric more easily if fabric is already anchored to the threads.

To chain piece, simply feed your patchwork units through the sewing machine one after the other without snipping the threads between them. Once you've finished sewing the units, cut the threads connecting them and press the seam allowances as instructed.

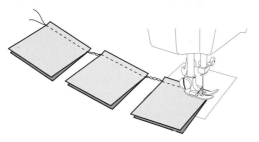

PRESSING SEAM ALLOWANCES

Careful pressing of seam allowances is very important. Poor pressing results in stretched and twisted seams. Good pressing results in pieces that lie nice and flat and are the correct size. The rule is to press seam allowances toward the darker fabric, where possible. You'll also want to have butted seams pressed in opposite directions; they'll nest together and match better than butted seams pressed in the same direction. Once you start sewing the quilt together, the rule is to iron the seam allowances toward the least bulky side. To attain all of these goals, some planning is necessary. Follow the instructions given for each project.

1. Place the unit you wish to press on the ironing board with the side that you want the seam allowances to go toward on the top.

2. With the two pieces still facing each other as they were sewn, briefly place the iron on top of the seam line to set the stitches.

3. Fold the top piece back and finger-press along the seam, making sure that the seam is not twisting but sitting flat.

4. Run the iron down the seam and let the heat from the iron do the job. It's not necessary to use a sawing action, because the iron's heat will press the seam, rather than the motion of the iron. The seam allowances will now lie underneath the fabric that was positioned on top.

QUICK CORNER TRIANGLES

Several of the designs in this book are pieced using the quick-corner-triangles method. This involves using a larger square or rectangle and a smaller square to produce a triangle or angled corner.

1. On the wrong side of the smaller square, draw a diagonal line from corner to corner.

2. Place the marked piece on one corner of the larger square or rectangle, right sides together. Sew on the drawn line.

3. Trim away the outside layers ¼" from the stitching line.

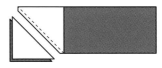

4. Press the resulting triangle away from the larger piece.

Several of the designs will also have another square sewn to the opposite side of the larger piece, but the

angle of the resulting triangle will run in the opposite direction.

HALF-SQUARE-TRIANGLE UNITS

This method of making half-square-triangle units minimizes stretching the bias edge of the squares and produces two half-square triangles for each pair of squares used.

1. Cut two contrasting squares to the size needed. Draw a diagonal line from corner to corner on the wrong side of the lighter-colored square.

2. Place the squares right sides together with the marked square on top and the edges aligned.

3. Sew ¼" from both sides of the drawn line.

4. Cut on the drawn line to create two half-square-triangle units. Press the seam allowances toward the darker fabric in each unit.

QUILTING

We've used a variety of quilting styles on the designs in this book. Some are quilted on our long-arm machine; other projects are hand quilted. Choose whichever method you prefer.

BINDING

Unless indicated, binding strips are cut across the width of the fabric and attached to the quilt top to make a double-fold binding.

1. Follow the cutting instructions for each pattern to cut the required number of 2½"-wide strips.

2. Join the strips end to end using a diagonal seam, and then trim away the excess fabric ¼" from the stitching lines. Press the seam allowances open.

3. Press the beginning end of the strip at a 45° angle. Fold the fabric in half lengthwise, wrong sides together, and press the binding flat.

4. Beginning with the angled end, pin the binding to one side of the quilt top, aligning the raw edges. Using a ¼" seam allowance, begin sewing approximately 3" from the angled end and stop sewing ¼" from the first corner; backstitch.

5. Remove the quilt from the sewing machine. Fold the binding up at a 90° angle, and then bring it back down onto itself to square the corner. Begin stitching at the edge of the binding strip and stop sewing ¼" from the next corner. Repeat the folding and sewing process for each corner.

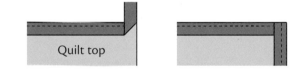

6. Keep sewing until you reach the beginning of the binding strip. Lap the end of the binding strip over the beginning about 2"; cut off the excess.

7. Tuck the tail of the binding inside the fold of the angled end, and then continue sewing until you reach the point where you began stitching; backstitch.

8. Fold the binding to the back of the quilt and pin it in place. Hand slipstitch the fold of the binding to the back of the quilt.

I love the look of an appliqué surrounded by a dogtooth border, so when I designed this charming vase of flowers, I included those details. Fond memories of my youngest daughter, Jess, collecting flowers for me when she was little inspired this piece. A purchased wooden frame finishes off the piece nicely.

— Leonie

Designed, hand appliquéd, and hand quilted by Leonie Bateman

Unframed Finished Piece: 16" x 20"

MATERIALS

Silk Fabric

20" x 22" piece of beige silk matka or linen for background

Felted Wool Fabric

Yardage is based on 48"-wide fabric.

7" x 22" piece of pumpkin orange for dogtooth border

10" x 12" piece of forest green for stems

6" x 11" piece of aubergine for feathery leaves, small flowers, small-flower reverse-appliqué inserts, and berries

6½" x 7½" piece of dusty pink plaid for flowers

6½" x 7" piece of claret for pot

5½" x 6½" piece of butterscotch for flowers and flower reverse-appliqué inserts

2" x 12" piece of medium green for leaves

1" x 12" piece of light green for leaves

Additional Materials

24"-long piece of freezer paper

Water-soluble glue stick

Stapler

Embroidery floss in colors to match wool fabrics

16" x 20" purchased frame (the front opening should be no smaller than 15½" x 19½")

CUTTING

From the forest-green wool, cut:

1 strip, ⅜" x 9"

2 strips, ⅜" x 5½"

2 *bias* strips, ⅜" x 8"

PREPARING FOR APPLIQUÉ

1. Fold the piece of beige silk or linen in half vertically and horizontally; finger-press the folds.

2. Measure the length and width of the front opening of your frame. Center and mark the opening measurements on your background fabric, keeping the rectangle centered. The easiest way to do this is to calculate half of the length. Find this measurement on your acrylic ruler and position that line on the horizontal fold line of the background fabric; mark across the top of the ruler. Continue across the horizontal line to mark the entire length across the top of the fabric. Repeat to measure and mark across the bottom of the fabric.

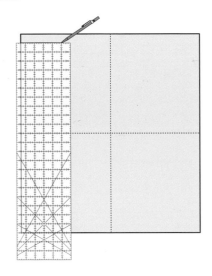

In the same manner, calculate half the width of the opening, measure from the vertical fold line, and mark down the sides of the background fabric. These will be your guidelines for placing the dogtooth-border appliqué pieces.

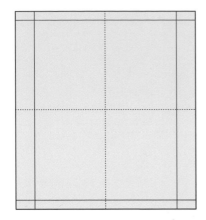

3. Refer to "Cutting the Border Strips" (page 8) to trace the dogtooth-border pattern on page 15 onto freezer paper, repeating the design to make a strip 22" long for a side border. Repeat to make one additional side border strip. In the same manner, make two freezer-paper border strips that measure 18" long. Use the freezer-paper patterns to cut the dogtooth-border strips from the pumpkin-orange wool.

ADDING THE APPLIQUÉS

1. Refer to "Positioning the Border Strips" (page 8) to place the dogtooth-border strips on the background fabric, making sure to align the inner points with the marked lines on the background. Glue and staple the borders in place.

2. Refer to "Making a Master Pattern" (page 6) to make a master pattern using the patterns on pages 16 and 17.

3. Refer to "Making the Appliqués" (page 6) to trace all of the appliqué shapes onto freezer paper, roughly cut out the shapes, and then iron the freezer-paper shapes onto your chosen colors of wool. Refer to the photo on page 12 and the materials list for fabric choices as needed. Cut out the wool shapes.

4. Refer to "Preassembling Units" (page 7) to assemble the large and small flower-bud appliqué shapes into units using reverse appliqué (page 9) for the cutout sections.

5. Lay your master pattern on a light box or other light source, and then position the prepared background fabric on top of the master pattern, lining up the center folds of the background with the reference lines on the master pattern. Pin the background to the master pattern.

6. Refer to "Appliquéing Wool to the Background" (page 7) to glue and staple your prepared appliqué pieces in place, working from the bottom layer to the top.

7. Using your thread and needle of choice, appliqué the pieces in place with a blanket stitch. Remove the staples.

FINISHING

To complete this project, I marked a diagonal crosshatch design with the lines spaced ½" apart through the pot using a ruler and white pencil, and then hand quilted the lines. This quilting creates a nice texture while anchoring the piece to the background. I also added quilting to the reverse-appliqué pieces to give them depth.

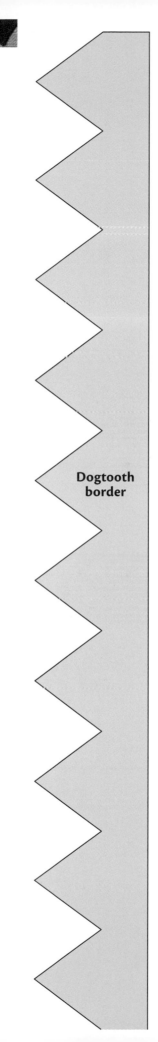

Dogtooth border

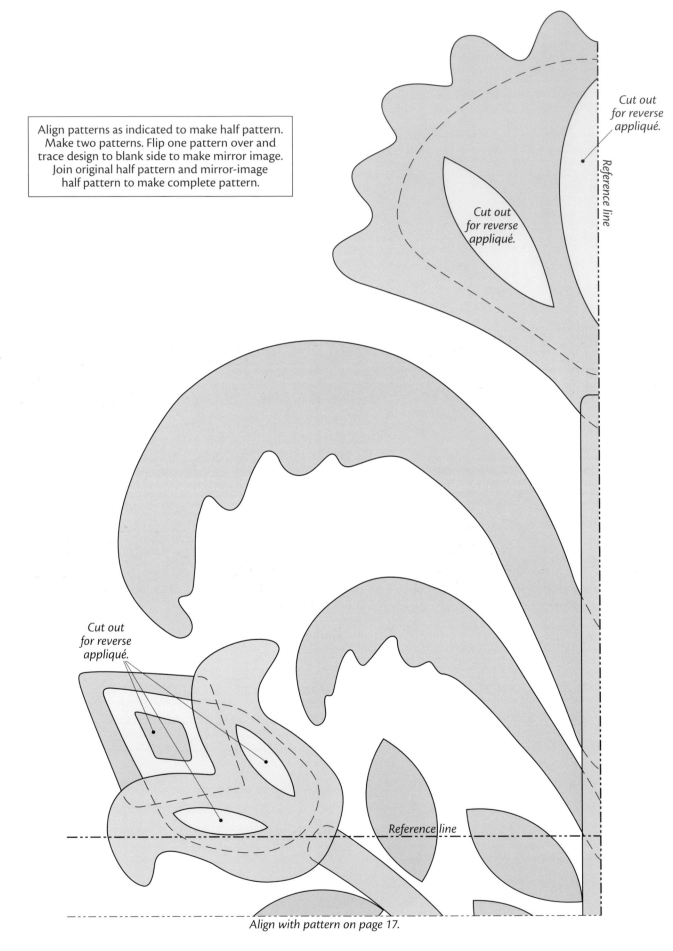

Align patterns as indicated to make half pattern. Make two patterns. Flip one pattern over and trace design to blank side to make mirror image. Join original half pattern and mirror-image half pattern to make complete pattern.

Cut out for reverse appliqué.

Reference line

Cut out for reverse appliqué.

Cut out for reverse appliqué.

Reference line

Align with pattern on page 17.

Align with pattern on page 16.

Reference line

Who can resist a pot overflowing with flowers handpicked from the garden in full bloom? Let this runner grace your table with appliquéd flowers from my garden. You may even want to hang it above a doorway or place it along the back of a sofa. However you choose to display it, it's sure to make a statement in your home.

— Leonie

Designed, hand appliquéd,
and hand quilted by Leonie Bateman
Finished Runner: 49" x 14"

MATERIALS

Cotton Fabric

Yardage is based on 42"-wide fabric.

1⅝ yards of gold print for background and backing

⅓ yard of red print for binding

Felted Wool Fabric

Yardage is based on 48"-wide fabric.

12" x 21" piece of green for main stems and 4 small leaves

10" x 12" piece of green large-scale plaid for center stem, 2 large leaves, and 6 small leaves

8½" x 10½" piece of tomato-red print for main flower and 4 small flowers

8½" x 10½" piece of gold print for main-flower and small-flower reverse-appliqué inserts, and base of teal flowers

9" x 10" piece of teal for fanned flowers

5" x 9½" piece of brown print for pot

2" x 7" piece of aubergine for berries

3" x 5" piece of green herringbone for 2 small leaves

3" x 5" piece of green flecked for 2 small leaves

Additional Materials

16" x 51" piece of batting

40"-long piece of freezer paper

Water-soluble glue stick

Stapler

Embroidery floss in colors to match wool fabrics

CUTTING

From the *lengthwise grain* of the gold cotton print, cut:
2 strips, 16" x 51"

From the red print, cut:
4 strips, 2½" x 42"

PREPARING FOR APPLIQUÉ

1. Fold one of the gold strips in half vertically; finger-press the fold line. Set aside the remaining gold strip for the backing. Using the marking tool of your choice, mark a guideline 1½" above the bottom edge of the background strip.

2. Refer to "Making a Master Pattern" (page 6) to make a master pattern using the patterns on pages 21–24.

3. Refer to "Making the Appliqués" (page 6) to trace all of the appliqué shapes onto freezer paper, and then iron the freezer-paper shapes onto your chosen colors of wool. Refer to the photo on page 18 and the materials list for fabric choices as needed. Cut out the wool shapes.

4. Refer to "Reverse Appliqué" (page 9) to reverse appliqué the cutout sections of the large and small red flowers.

5. Lay your master pattern on a light box or other light source, and then position the prepared background fabric on top of the master pattern, lining up the vertical center fold of the background

with the reference line on the master pattern. The bottom of the pot should line up with the marked line you drew in step 1. Pin the background to the master pattern.

ADDING THE APPLIQUÉS

1. Refer to "Appliquéing Wool to the Background" (page 7) to glue and staple your prepared appliqué pieces in place, working from the bottom layer to the top.

2. Using your thread and needle of choice, appliqué the pieces in place with a blanket stitch. Remove the staples.

FINISHING

1. Sandwich the batting between the runner top and the gold 16" x 51" backing piece, and then baste the layers together.

2. Quilt as desired. I marked a diagonal crosshatch design with the lines spaced 2" apart throughout the entire project using a white pencil, and then hand quilted over the lines. I also added quilting to the reverse-appliqué pieces to give them depth.

3. Trim the runner to measure 49" x 14", keeping the design centered.

4. Refer to "Binding" (page 11) to bind the table-runner edges with the red 2½"-wide strips.

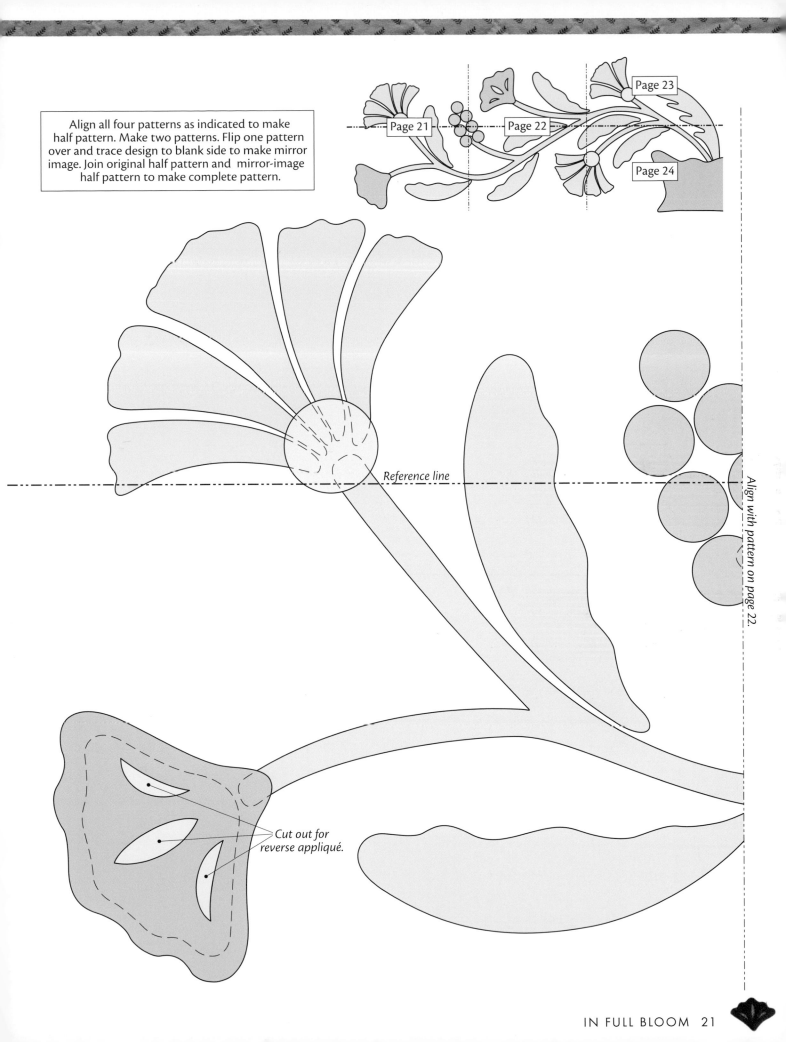

Align all four patterns as indicated to make half pattern. Make two patterns. Flip one pattern over and trace design to blank side to make mirror image. Join original half pattern and mirror-image half pattern to make complete pattern.

Page 21 Page 22 Page 23 Page 24

Reference line

Align with pattern on page 22.

Cut out for reverse appliqué.

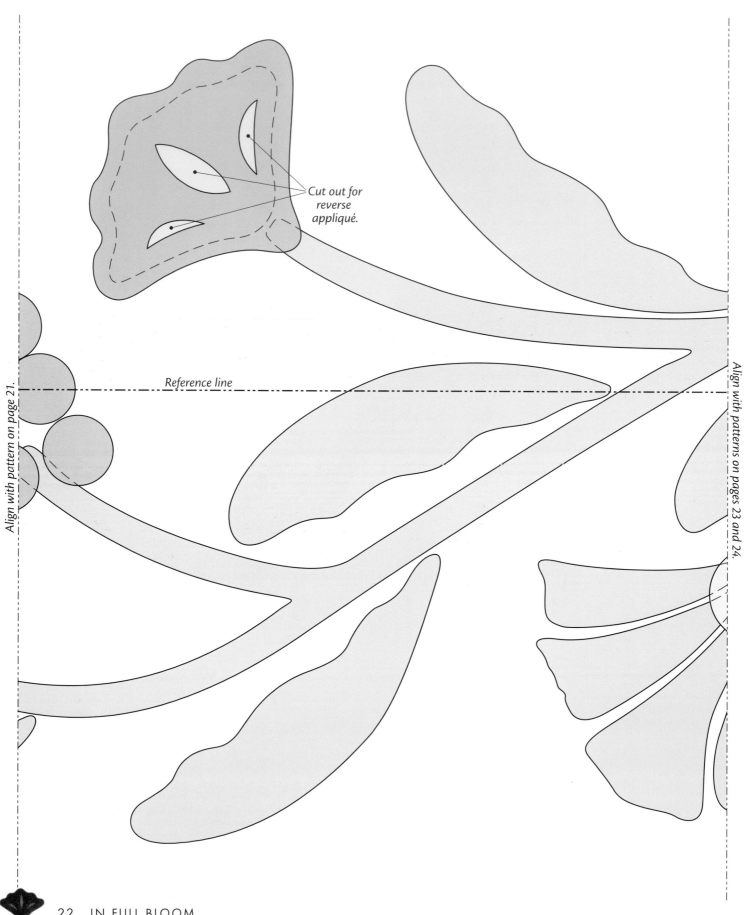

Cut out for
reverse
appliqué.

Reference line

Align with pattern on page 21.

Align with patterns on pages 23 and 24.

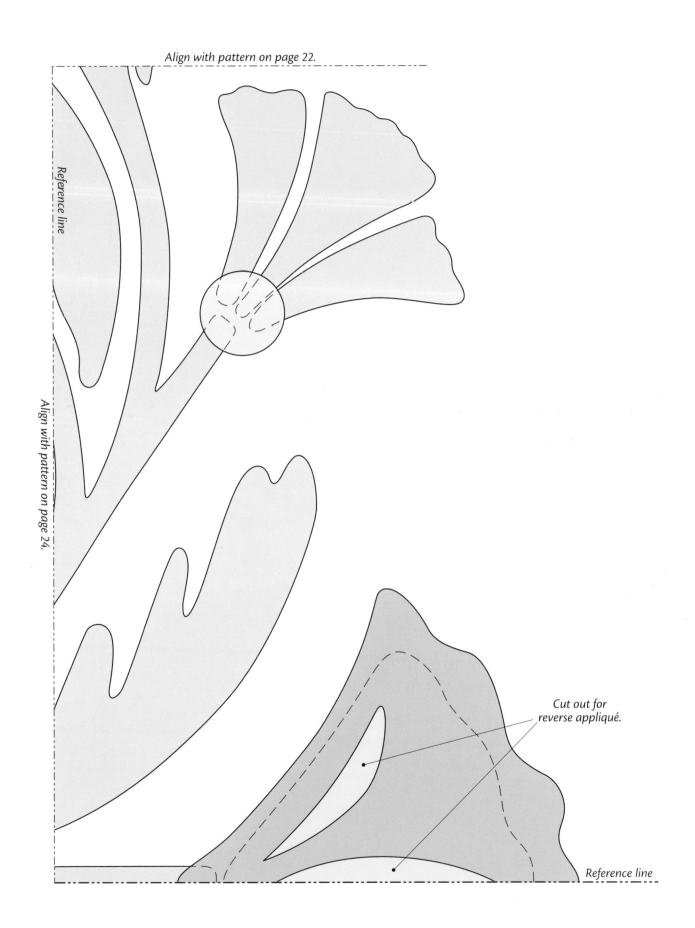

Align with pattern on page 22.

Reference line

Align with pattern on page 24.

Cut out for reverse appliqué.

Reference line

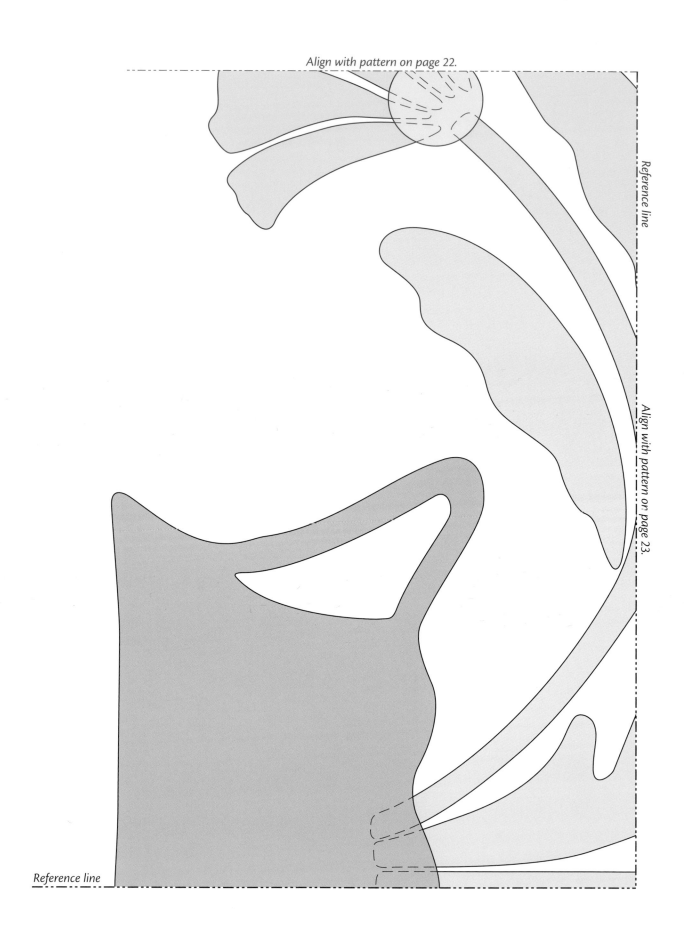

Align with pattern on page 22.

Reference line

Align with pattern on page 23.

Reference line

> Enjoy making this delightful cushion featuring birds sitting on a branch surrounded by flowers. I turned my appliqué design into a lovely pillow, but you may choose to place the finished appliqué in a frame or turn it into a quilted wall hanging.
>
> – *Leonie*

Designed, hand appliquéd, and hand quilted by Leonie Bateman

Finished Pillow: 27¾" x 17¾"

MATERIALS

Cotton Fabric

Yardage is based on 42"-wide fabric.

1½ yards of black tone-on-tone print for pillow front and back

1⅛ yards of muslin for pillow form

Felted Wool Fabric

Yardage is based on 48"-wide fabric.

7" x 23" piece of deep pink for scalloped edge and base of flowers

2½" x 5" piece of medium pink for flower centers

2" x 5" piece of light pink for flower tips

6" x 10" piece of green or scraps of assorted greens for leaves

7" x 8" piece of teal for bird bodies

4" x 4½" piece of light blue for bird wings

2½" x 7" piece of medium brown for branch

2" x 2" square of caramel for bird legs

Additional Materials

18¼" x 28¼" piece of fusible batting

24"-long piece of freezer paper

Water-soluble glue stick

Stapler

Embroidery floss in colors to match wool fabrics, plus brown for vines and birds' eyes

Polyester fiberfill

CUTTING

From the black tone-on-tone print, cut:

1 rectangle, 14½" x 21"

1 rectangle, 18¼" x 28¼"

1 strip, 5" x 42"; crosscut into 2 rectangles, 5" x 12¼"

2 strips, 3½" x 28¼"

From the muslin, cut:

2 rectangles, 18¼" x 28¼"

PREPARING FOR APPLIQUÉ

1. Fold the black 14½" x 21" rectangle in half vertically and horizontally; finger-press the folds. Using a white marking tool or the marking tool of your choice, mark the fold lines.

2. Measure 5¾" from both sides of the horizontal centerline and mark a line parallel to the top and bottom edges. Measure 9¼" from the vertical centerline in both directions and mark a line parallel to the side edges.

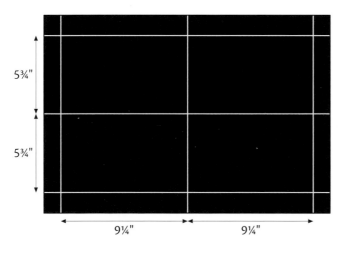

3. Refer to "Cutting the Border Strips" (page 8) to trace the scalloped-border pattern on page 28 onto freezer paper, repeating the design to make a strip 17" long for a side border. Repeat to make one additional side-border strip. In the same manner, make two freezer-paper border strips that measure 23" long for the top and bottom border strips. Use the freezer-paper templates to cut the scalloped-border strips from the deep-pink wool.

4. Refer to "Positioning the Border Strips" (page 8) to place the border strips on the background fabric,

aligning the inner points with the marked lines on the background. Glue and staple the borders in place.

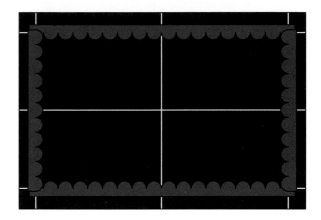

5. Trim the border strips ⅜" from the inner points. Your piece should now measure 12¼" x 19¼".

6. Using a ¼" seam allowance, sew the black 5" x 12¼" rectangles to the sides of the pillow-cover top. Press the seam allowances toward the rectangles. Add the 3½" x 28¼" strips to the top and bottom of the pillow-cover top. Press the seam allowances toward the strips.

7. Refer to "Making a Master Pattern" (page 6) to make a master pattern using the patterns on pages 29–31.

8. Refer to "Making the Appliqués" (page 6) to trace all of the appliqué shapes onto freezer paper, roughly cut them out, and then iron the freezer-paper shapes onto your chosen colors of wool. Refer to the photo on page 25 and the materials list for fabric choices as needed. Cut out the wool shapes.

9. Refer to "Preassembling Units" on page 7 to assemble the flower pieces and bird pieces into units.

ADDING THE APPLIQUÉS

1. Refer to "Appliquéing Wool to the Background" (page 7) to position the appliqués on the background fabric, working from the bottom layer to the top. Because you're working with a dark background fabric, use the marked reference lines on your background to help you place the appliqués. Glue and staple the appliqués in place.

2. Once your appliqués are positioned, use a white pencil and hand draw the vines. Use a Pekinese stitch (page 7) and two strands of your chosen thread to embroider the vines.

3. Using the thread and needle of your choice, appliqué the pieces in place with a blanket stitch. Use a satin stitch (page 7) for the birds' eyes. Remove the staples.

FINISHING

1. Follow the manufacturer's instructions to fuse the batting to the wrong side of the pillow-cover top.

2. Quilt as desired. I quilted diagonal lines 1" apart through the borders, and outline quilted the center appliqués.

3. Lay the pillow-cover front and the black 18¼" x 28¼" back right sides together. Use the corner trimming pattern on page 31 to make a template and use it to round off the pillow-cover corners. Pin the front and back together.

4. Stitch the front to the back, leaving a 14" opening along the bottom edge. Turn the pillow cover right side out.

5. To make the pillow form, lay the muslin rectangles on top of each other, aligning the edges. Use the corner trimming template to round off the corners. Stitch the muslin pieces together, leaving an opening for inserting the stuffing. Firmly stuff the form with fiberfill, and then sew the opening closed. Insert the pillow form through the pillow-cover opening. Sew the opening closed.

Adding a Zipper

If you think you might want to remove the pillow form at some point, adding a zipper to the pillow cover will make it easier to do so. Follow the package instructions to apply a 20"-long zipper in the bottom seam line of the cover before you sew the front and back completely together.

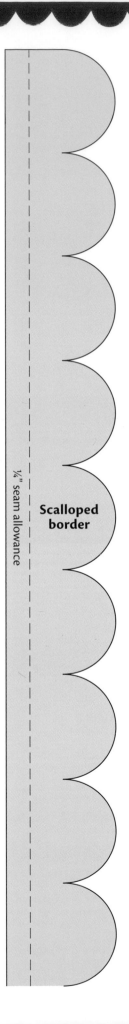

¼" seam allowance

Scalloped border

Embroidery
placement

Reference line

Align with pattern on page 30.

Embroidery
placement

Reference line

Align with pattern on page 29.

Align with pattern on page 31.

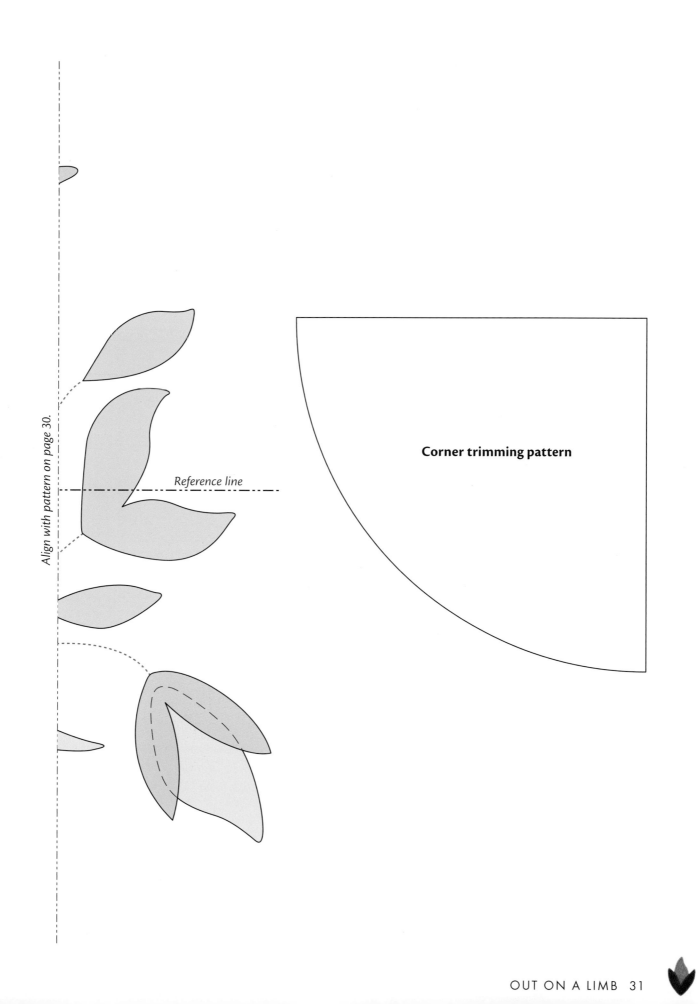

Align with pattern on page 30.

Reference line

Corner trimming pattern

After completing "Poppy's Quilt," my four-block appliqué quilt shown on page 38, I thought it would be fun to see how different an appliqué block could look with a change of colors and a different sort of pieced border. As you can see, the result is a block that looks completely different but just as stunning. This is my eldest daughter Ellen's favorite piece—she really loves this one!

— Leonie

Designed, machine pieced, hand appliquéd, and machine quilted by Leonie Bateman

Finished Quilt: 30" x 30"

MATERIALS

Cotton Fabric

Yardage is based on 42"-wide fabric.

1¼ yards of dark-teal print for background and pieced border

5" x 20" piece of red-and-black print for cornerstones

5" x 6" piece each of 22 assorted cotton prints in pinks, blues, browns, reds, and tans for pieced border

⅜ yard of brown print for binding

1¼ yards of fabric for backing

Felted Wool Fabric

Yardage is based on 48"-wide fabric.

½ yard of deep red for large and small fanned flowers and small center circle

10" x 20" piece of brown for stems and leaves

6½" x 6½" square of light-teal herringbone for center flower and base of large and small flowers

2½" x 2½" square of dark-brown print for large center circle

Additional Materials

38" x 38" piece of batting

35"-long piece of freezer paper

Water-soluble glue stick

Stapler

Embroidery floss in colors to match wool fabrics

CUTTING

From the dark-teal print, cut:

6 strips, 2½" x 42"; crosscut into 88 squares, 2½" x 2½"

1 square, 22½" x 22½"

From the red-and-black print, cut:

4 squares, 4½" x 4½"

From *each* of the 22 assorted prints, cut:

2 rectangles, 2½" x 4½" (44 total)

From the brown print for binding, cut:

4 strips, 2½" x 42"

PREPARING FOR APPLIQUÉ

1. Mark a diagonal line from corner to corner on the wrong side of each dark-teal 2½" square. Refer to "Quick Corner Triangles" (page 10) to place a marked square on one end of an assorted-print 2½" x 4½" rectangle, right sides together. Sew on the marked line. Trim the seam allowances to ¼". Press the triangle toward the corner. Repeat on the opposite end of the rectangle. Repeat to make a total of 44 flying-geese units.

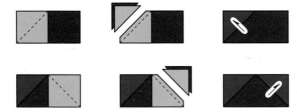

Make 44.

2. Sew 11 flying-geese units together along the long edges, with the points going in the same direction as shown, to make a border strip. Press the seam allowances in one direction. Repeat to make a total of four border strips.

Make 4.

3. Sew a flying-geese border strip to each side of the dark-teal 22½" center square. Press the seam allowances toward the center square. Sew a red-and-black 4½" square to each end of the remaining two border strips. Press the seam allowances toward the squares. Join these strips to the top and bottom of the center square. Press the seam allowances toward the center square.

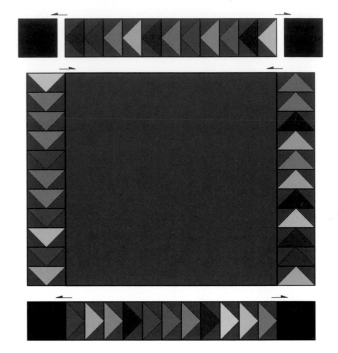

4. Fold the quilt top in half vertically and horizontally and finger-press the folds. Fold the quilt top in half diagonally in each direction and finger-press the folds. Use a white marking tool or other tool of your choice to mark over the folds. Because you're working with a dark background fabric, these lines will be used as guidelines to help position the appliqués.

5. Refer to "Making a Master Pattern" (page 6) to make a master pattern using the quarter pattern on pages 36 and 37.

6. Refer to "Making the Appliqués" (page 6) to trace all of the appliqué shapes onto freezer paper, roughly cut out the shapes, and then iron the freezer-paper shapes onto your chosen colors of wool. Refer to the photo on page 32 and the materials list for fabric choices as needed. Cut out the wool shapes.

7. Refer to "Preassembling Units" (page 7) to assemble the center-flower pieces into a unit.

ADDING THE APPLIQUÉS

1. Refer to "Appliquéing Wool to the Background" (page 7) to position the appliqués on the background fabric, working from the bottom layer to the top. Because you're working with a dark background fabric, use the marked reference lines on your background to help you place the appliqués. Glue and staple the appliqués in place.

2. Using your thread and needle of choice, appliqué the pieces in place using a blanket stitch. Remove the staples.

FINISHING

1. Cut the backing fabric so it's 4" larger than the quilt top on each side. Sandwich the batting between the backing and quilt top, and baste the layers together.

2. Quilt as desired. I quilted my top on my long-arm quilting machine.

3. Trim the backing and batting even with the quilt top. Refer to "Binding" (page 11) to bind the quilt edges with the brown 2½"-wide strips.

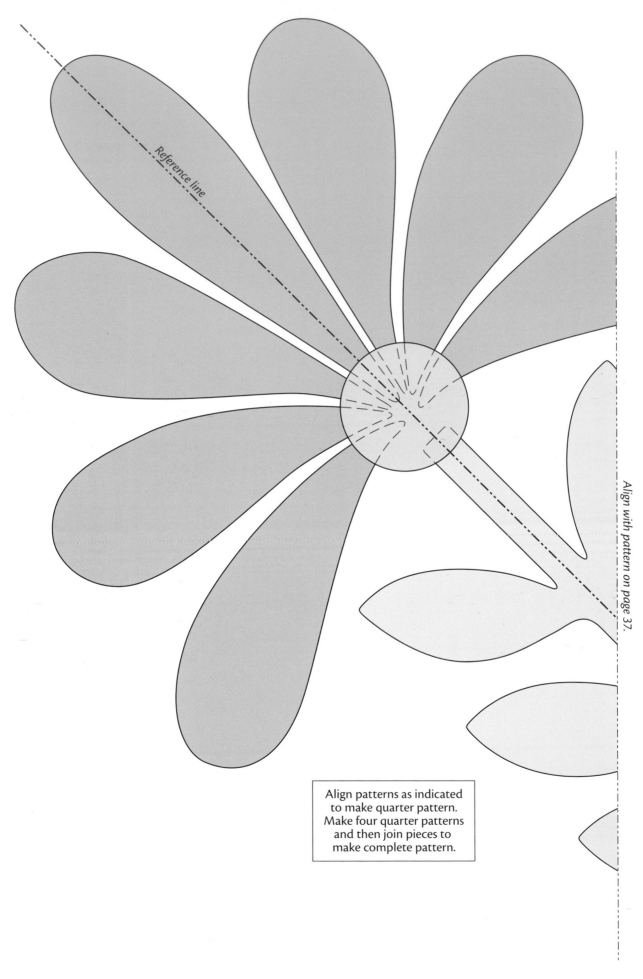

Reference line

Align with pattern on page 37.

Align patterns as indicated
to make quarter pattern.
Make four quarter patterns
and then join pieces to
make complete pattern.

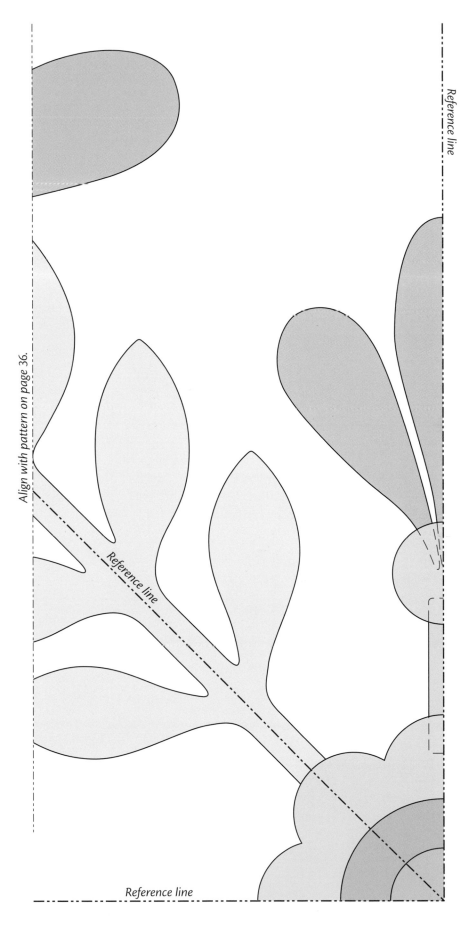

Align with pattern on page 36.

Reference line

Reference line

Reference line

Poppy's Quilt

This four-block appliqué was inspired by those from the 1800s. Wool appliqué is featured in the large blocks, while square-in-a-square units—pieced from a favorite range of fabrics from my stash—form the sashing. I thoroughly enjoyed making this beauty and hope that you get the same amount of pleasure from it that I did. The quilt is named after our cat, Poppy, who always managed to curl up in it when I needed to stitch!

— *Leonie*

Designed, machine pieced, hand appliquéd, and hand quilted by Leonie Bateman
Finished Quilt: 52" x 52"

MATERIALS

Cotton Fabric

Yardage is based on 42"-wide fabric.

2⅞ yards of shirting print for appliquéd-block backgrounds and sashing

⅓ yard *each* of 8 assorted red prints for sashing and large-leaf reverse-appliqué inserts

½ yard of red print for binding

3½ yards of fabric for backing

Felted Wool Fabric

Yardage is based on 48"-wide fabric.

16" x 48" piece of deep red for large and small fanned flowers and scalloped-flower center circles

20" x 32" piece of green for stems, small leaves, and scalloped-flower inner circles

14" x 20" piece of gold for scalloped flowers and base of fanned flowers

14" x 18" piece of gray for pots

9" x 24" piece of green plaid for large leaves

Additional Materials

60" x 60" piece of batting

60"-long piece of freezer paper

Water-soluble glue stick

Stapler

Embroidery floss in colors to match wool fabrics

CUTTING

From the shirting print, cut:

4 squares, 22" x 22"

276 squares, 2½" x 2½"

From *each* of the 8 assorted red prints, cut:

2 strips, 4½" x 42"; crosscut into 9 squares,
4½" x 4½" (72 total; you'll have 3 squares left over)

From the red print for binding, cut:

6 strips, 2½" x 42"

PREPARING FOR APPLIQUÉ

1. Fold each shirting-print 22" square in half vertically
   and horizontally and finger-press the folds. Fold
   each square in half diagonally in both directions
   and finger-press the folds. If desired, mark over the
   fold lines with a water-soluble marker.

2. Refer to "Making a Master Pattern" (page 6) to
   make a master pattern using the patterns on pages
   42–45.

3. Refer to "Making the Appliqués" (page 6) to trace
   all of the appliqué shapes onto freezer paper,
   roughly cut out the shapes, and then iron the
   freezer-paper shapes onto your chosen colors of
   wool. You'll need four sets of appliqué shapes for
   the blocks. Refer to the photo on page 38 and the
   materials list for fabric choices as needed. Cut out
   the wool shapes.

4. Refer to "Preassembling Units" (page 7) to
   assemble the scalloped-flower pieces into a unit.
   Refer to "Reverse Appliqué" (page 9) to reverse
   appliqué the cutout sections of the large leaves
   with the remainder of one of the assorted red
   cotton prints.

ADDING THE APPLIQUÉS

1. Refer to "Appliquéing Wool to the Background"
   (page 7) to position the appliqués on each of
   the background squares, working from the
   bottom layer to the top. Glue and staple the
   appliqués in place.

2. Using your thread and needle of choice, appliqué
   the pieces in place using a blanket stitch. Remove
   the staples.

3. Trim the blocks to 20½" square, keeping the
   design centered.

MAKING THE SASHING SQUARES

Draw a diagonal line from corner to corner on the
wrong side of each shirting-print 2½" square. Refer to
"Quick Corner Triangles" (page 10) to place marked
squares on opposite corners of a red 4½" square. Sew
on the marked lines. Trim the seam allowances to ¼".

Press the triangles toward the corners. Repeat on the opposite two corners. Repeat to make a total of 69 square-in-a-square units.

Make 69.

ASSEMBLING THE QUILT TOP

1. Sew five square-in-a-square units together as shown to make a vertical sashing strip. Press the seam allowances in one direction. Repeat to make a total of six strips.

Make 6.

2. Alternately sew three sashing strips and two blocks together as shown. Press the seam allowances toward the blocks. Repeat to make a total of two block rows.

Make 2.

3. Refer to step 1 to sew 13 square-in-a-square units together to make a horizontal sashing strip. Repeat to make a total of three strips.

4. Alternately sew the horizontal sashing strips and block rows together to complete the quilt top. Press the seam allowances toward the block rows.

FINISHING

1. Cut and piece the backing fabric so it's 4" larger than the quilt top on each side. Sandwich the batting between the backing and quilt top, and baste the layers together.

2. Quilt as desired.

3. Trim the backing and batting even with the quilt top. Refer to "Binding" (page 11) to bind the quilt edges with the red 2½"-wide strips.

Align all four patterns as indicated to make half pattern. Make two patterns. Flip one pattern over and trace design to blank side to make mirror image. Join original half pattern and mirror-image half pattern to make complete pattern.

Page 42

Page 43

Page 44

Page 45

¼" seam allowance

Reference line

Align with pattern on page 43.

Align with pattern on page 42.

Reference line

Reference line

Reference line

Align with pattern on page 44.

Reference line

Align with pattern on page 45.

¼" seam allowance

Reference line

Align with pattern on page 43.

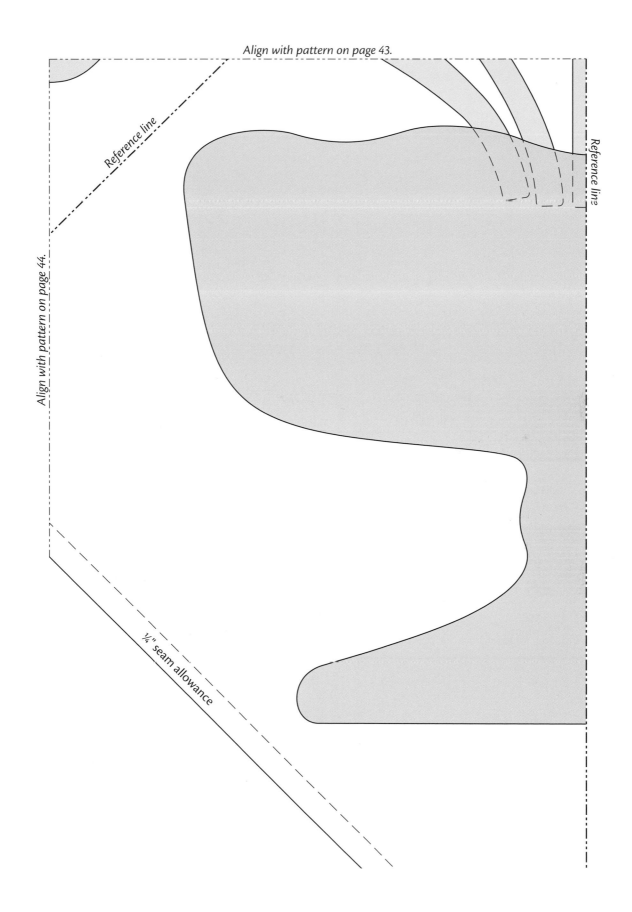

Align with pattern on page 43.

Reference line

Reference line

Align with pattern on page 44.

¼" seam allowance

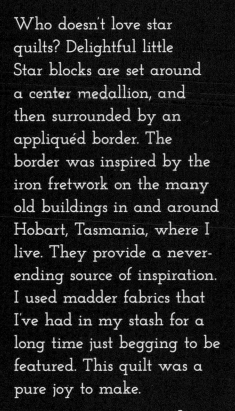

Who doesn't love star quilts? Delightful little Star blocks are set around a center medallion, and then surrounded by an appliquéd border. The border was inspired by the iron fretwork on the many old buildings in and around Hobart, Tasmania, where I live. They provide a never-ending source of inspiration. I used madder fabrics that I've had in my stash for a long time just begging to be featured. This quilt was a pure joy to make.

— Leonie

Designed, machine pieced, hand appliquéd, and machine quilted by Leonie Bateman

Finished Quilt: 54" x 54"

MATERIALS

Cotton Fabric

Yardage is based on 42"-wide fabric.

⅜ yard *each* of 7 assorted red prints for large and small Star blocks and flower reverse-appliqué inserts

2⅝ yards of shirting print for large and small Star blocks and appliquéd outer border

¾ yard of red print for plain squares

⅞ yard of brown print for inner border and binding

3¾ yards of fabric for backing

Felted Wool Fabric

Yardage is based on 48"-wide fabric.

20" x 48" piece of tan for stems and leaves

18" x 22" piece of rust for large and small fan flowers

8" x 20" piece of claret for pot and tulips

8" x 14" piece of brown herringbone for dogtooth border

5" x 8" piece of butterscotch for bird wings and tips of tulips

6" x 6" square of gold for bird bodies

Additional Materials

62" x 62" square of batting

60"-long piece of freezer paper

Water-soluble glue stick

Stapler

Embroidery floss in colors to match wool fabrics

CUTTING

From the *lengthwise grain* of the shirting print, cut:

4 strips, 10" x 40"

From the remainder of the shirting print, cut:

6 strips, 1½" x 42"; crosscut into 144 squares, 1½" x 1½"

7 strips, 2½" x 42"; crosscut into:

    144 rectangles, 1½" x 2½"

    16 squares, 2½" x 2½"

1 strip, 4½" x 42"; crosscut into 16 rectangles, 2½" x 4½"

1 square, 14" x 14"

From the tan wool, cut:

1 strip, ⅜" x 4½"

2 strips, ⅜" x 4"

12 *bias* strips, ⅜" x 24"

From *each* of 4 of the assorted red prints, cut:

8 squares, 2½" x 2½" (32 total)

1 square, 4½" x 4½" (4 total)

From the remainder of the assorted red prints, cut:

36 sets of 1 square, 2½" x 2½", and 8 matching squares, 1½" x 1½"

From the red print for plain squares, cut:

5 strips, 4½" x 42"; crosscut into 36 squares, 4½" x 4½"

From the brown print, cut:

2 strips, 1½" x 36½"

2 strips, 1½" x 38½"

7 strips, 2½" x 42"

PREPARING FOR APPLIQUÉ

1. Fold the shirting-print 14" square in half vertically and horizontally and finger-press the folds. Fold the shirting-print 10" x 40" strips in half vertically and horizontally and finger-press the folds. Use a water-soluble marker or the marking tool of your choice to mark over the fold lines.

2. On the 14" square, measure 6" from the marked horizontal line in both directions and mark a line parallel to the side edges. Measure 6" from the marked vertical line in both directions and mark a line parallel to the top and bottom edges. These will be your guidelines for placing your dogtooth-border pieces.

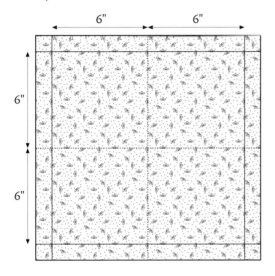

3. Refer to "Cutting the Border Strips" (page 8) and use the pattern on page 52 to make four 14"-long dogtooth-border strips from the brown-herringbone wool.

4. Refer to "Positioning the Border Strips" (page 8) to place the dogtooth-border strips on the center square, aligning the inner points with the marked lines on the background. Glue and staple the borders in place.

5. Refer to "Making a Master Pattern" (page 6) to make a master pattern of the center square using the pattern on page 53.

6. Make a master pattern of the outer border using the patterns on pages 54 and 55.

7. Refer to "Making the Appliqués" (page 6) to trace all of the appliqué shapes for the center square and outer border, except for the stems, onto freezer paper; roughly cut out the shapes, and then iron the freezer-paper shapes onto your chosen colors of wool. You'll need four sets of appliqués for the outer border. Refer to the photo on page 48 and the materials list for fabric choices as needed. Cut out the wool shapes.

8. Refer to "Preassembling Units" (page 7) to assemble the tulip appliqué shapes into units. Refer to "Reverse Appliqué" (page 9) to reverse appliqué the cutout sections of the large and small fan flowers using the leftover fabric from one of the assorted red prints.

ADDING THE APPLIQUÉS

1. Lay the master pattern for the center square on a light box or other light source, and then position the prepared background fabric on top of the master pattern, aligning the reference lines on the pattern and fabric. Pin the background to the master pattern.

2. Refer to "Appliquéing Wool to the Background" (page 7) to glue and staple your prepared appliqué pieces in place, using the tan ⅜" x 4½" strip for the center stem and the tan ⅜" x 4" strips for the side stems. Work from the bottom layer to the top when placing the appliqués.

3. Using your thread and needle of choice, appliqué the pieces in place with a blanket stitch. Use a satin stitch (page 7) for the birds' eyes. Remove the staples.

4. Trim the center square ¼" from the inner points of the dogtooth-border strips to make a piece 12½" x 12½".

5. Repeat steps 1–3 with the master pattern for the outer border and each of the border strips using the tan ⅜" x 24" strips for the stems. Trim the border strips to 8½" x 38½".

MAKING THE STAR BLOCKS

1. Mark a diagonal line from corner to corner on the wrong side of each assorted red 1½" square. Refer to "Quick Corner Triangles" (page 10) to place a marked square on one end of a shirting-print 1½" x 2½" rectangle. Sew on the marked line. Trim the seam allowances to ¼". Press the triangle toward the corner. Repeat on the opposite end of the rectangle using a matching red square. Repeat to make a total of 144 flying-geese units.

Make 144.

2. Arrange four matching flying-geese units, a matching red 2½" square, and four shirting-print 1½" squares into three horizontal rows as shown. Sew the pieces in each row together. Press the seam allowances toward the squares. Sew the rows together. Press the seam allowances toward the center row. Repeat to make a total of 36 small Star blocks.

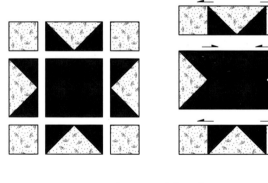

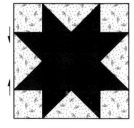

Make 36.

3. Repeat step 1 with the shirting-print 2½" x 4½" rectangles and assorted red 2½" squares to make 16 flying-geese units. Repeat step 2 using the flying-geese units, the matching red 4½" squares, and the shirting-print 2½" squares to make four large Star blocks.

ASSEMBLING THE QUILT TOP

1. Arrange five small Star blocks and four red 4½" plain squares into three horizontal rows. Sew the pieces in each row together. Press the seam allowances toward the plain squares. Sew the rows together. Press the seam allowances toward the middle row. Repeat to make a total of four of block A.

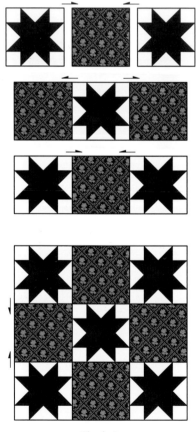

Block A.
Make 4.

2. Repeat step 1 using five red 4½" plain squares and four small Star blocks to make four of block B.

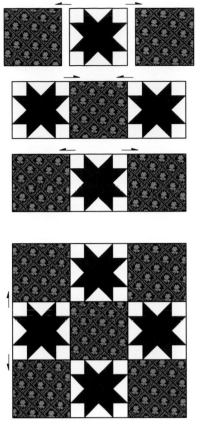

Block B.
Make 4.

3. Arrange the A and B blocks and the center
appliquéd block into three horizontal rows of three
blocks each as shown. Sew the blocks in each row
together. Press the seam allowances toward the
B blocks. Sew the rows together. Press the seam
allowances in one direction.

4. Sew the brown-print 1½" x 36½" strips to the sides
of the quilt top. Press the seam allowances toward
the border strips. Sew the brown-print 1½" x 38½"
strips to the top and bottom of the quilt top. Press
the seam allowances toward the border strips.
Your quilt top must measure 38½" x 38½" in order
for the outer-border strips to fit.

5. Refer to the photo on page 48 and the quilt
assembly diagram to sew the outer borders to the
sides of the quilt top. Press the seam allowances
toward the inner border. Add a large Star block to
each end of the remaining two outer-border strips.
Press the seam allowances toward the blocks. Sew
the strips to the top and bottom of the quilt top.
Press the seam allowances toward the inner border.

Quilt assembly

FINISHING

1. Cut and piece the backing fabric so it's 4" larger
than the quilt top on each side. Sandwich the
batting between the backing and quilt top, and
baste the layers together.

2. Quilt as desired. I chose to quilt an allover design
using my long-arm machine.

3. Trim the backing and batting even with the quilt
top. Refer to "Binding" (page 11) to bind the quilt
edges with the brown 2½"-wide strips.

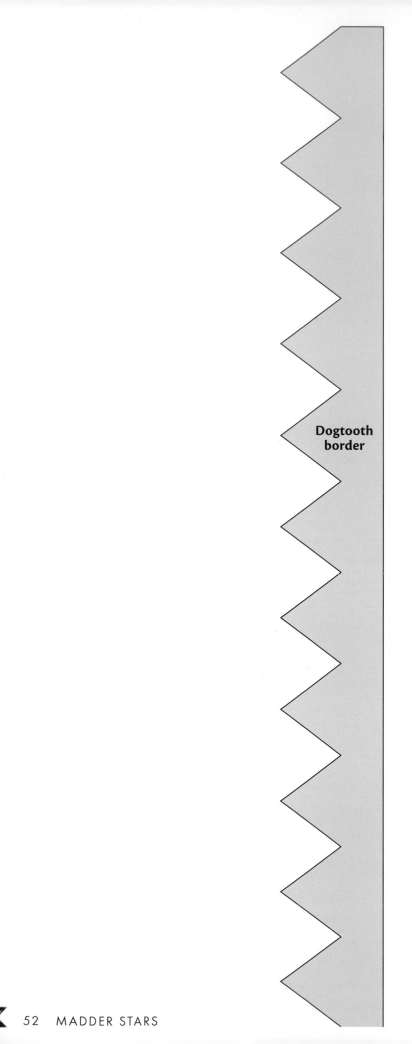

Dogtooth border

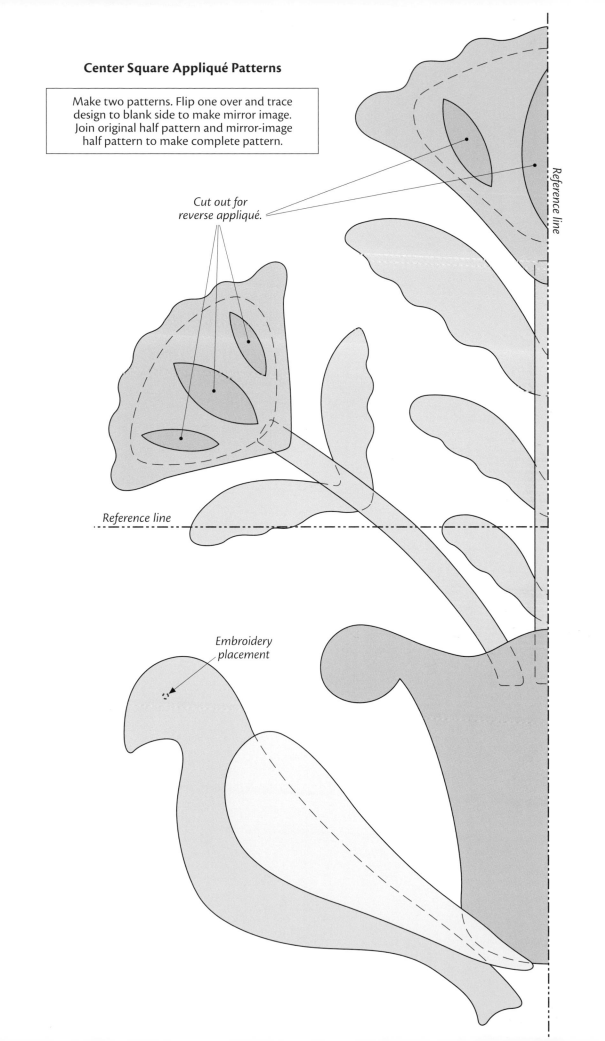

Center Square Appliqué Patterns

Make two patterns. Flip one over and trace design to blank side to make mirror image. Join original half pattern and mirror-image half pattern to make complete pattern.

Cut out for reverse appliqué.

Reference line

Reference line

Embroidery placement

53

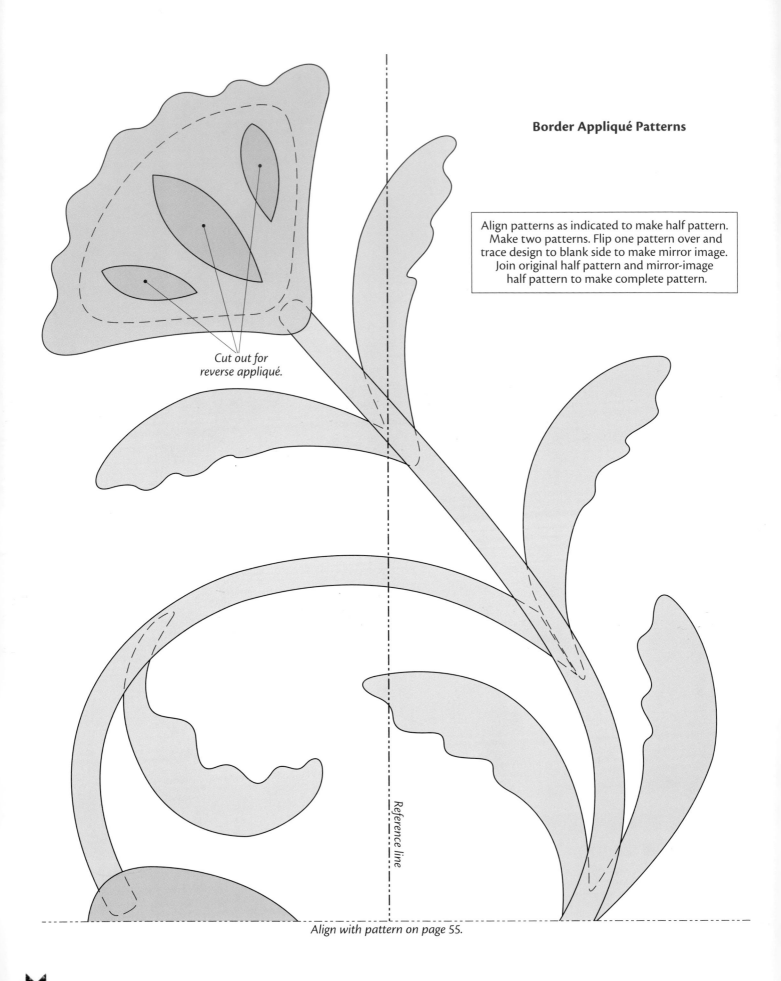

Border Appliqué Patterns

Align patterns as indicated to make half pattern. Make two patterns. Flip one pattern over and trace design to blank side to make mirror image. Join original half pattern and mirror-image half pattern to make complete pattern.

Cut out for reverse appliqué.

Reference line

Align with pattern on page 55.

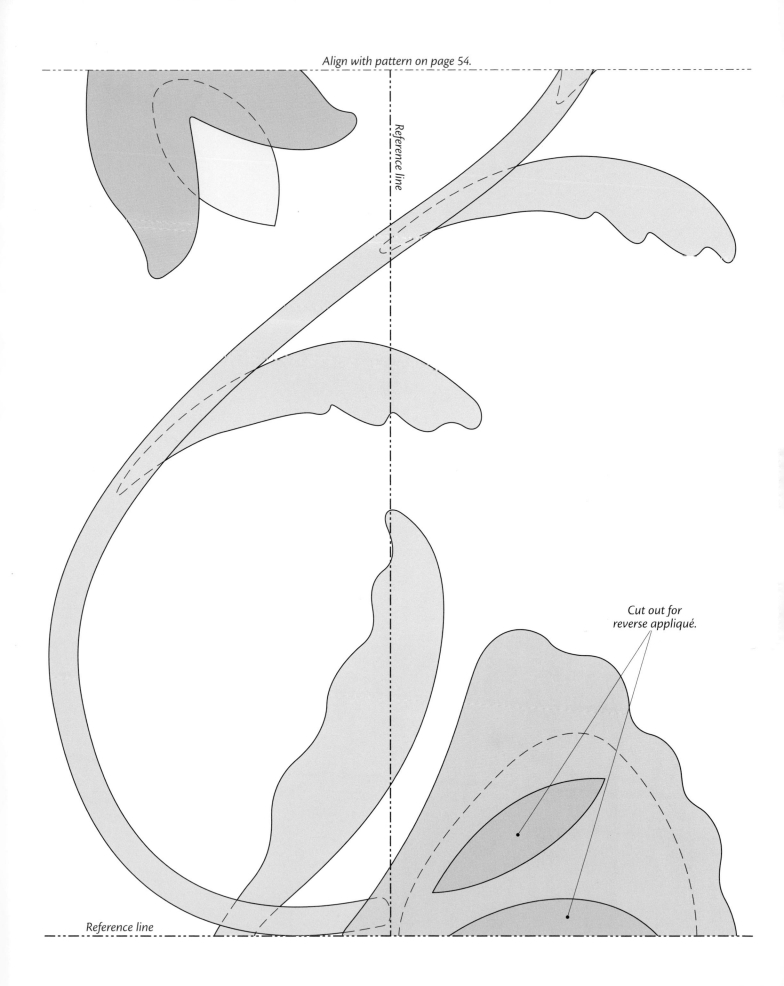

Reference line

Cut out for
reverse appliqué.

Reference line

I combined my love of piecing (in this case Checkerboard blocks) with appliqué in this charming quilt. Traditional flowers and oak leaves with straight stems give the quilt an old-fashioned feel. Twenty-five different cotton prints and many different-colored pieces of felted wool give the quilt a delightfully scrappy look. When the appliqué and patchwork are combined, this colorful design reminds me of my daughter, Casey, and her whimsical style.

— Deirdre

Designed, machine pieced, hand appliquéd, and machine quilted by Deirdre Bond-Abel

Finished Quilt: 45½" x 45½"

MATERIALS

Cotton Fabric

Yardage is based on 42"-wide fabric.

1⅞ yards of cream print for appliquéd-block backgrounds and border

1½" x 42" strip each of 25 assorted prints for Checkerboard blocks

½ yard of burgundy print for binding

3 yards of fabric for backing

Felted Wool Fabric

Yardage is based on 48"-wide fabric.

8" x 48" piece of tan for center-block and border leaves

6" x 48" piece of denim blue for center-block and border scalloped flowers

4" x 48" piece of burgundy for center-block and border stems

5" x 24" piece of dusty pink for center-block and border tulips

3" x 24" piece of cherry red for center-block and border scalloped-flower centers

2½" x 12" piece *each* of 20 assorted colors for small appliquéd-block leaves, scalloped flowers, and flower centers

Additional Materials

53" x 53" piece of batting

36"-long piece of freezer paper

Water-soluble glue stick

Embroidery floss or flower thread in colors to match wool fabrics

CUTTING

From the cream print, cut:

1 strip, 16" x 42"; crosscut into:

    1 square, 16" x 16"

    6 squares, 6" x 6"

7 strips, 6" x 42"; crosscut into:

    4 strips, 6" x 36"

    14 squares, 6" x 6"

From *each* of the 25 assorted-print strips, cut:

4 strips, 1½" x 10" (100 total)

From the burgundy wool, cut:

5 strips, ⅜" x 48"; crosscut into:

    4 strips, ⅜" x 32"

    20 rectangles, ⅜" x 2½"

    12 rectangles, ⅜" x 3"

    4 rectangles, ⅜" x 5"

From the burgundy print, cut:

5 strips, 2½" x 42"

MAKING THE CHECKERBOARD BLOCKS

1. Separate the assorted-print 1½" x 10" strips into 20 groups of five different strips each.

2. Sew the strips from one group together along their long edges. Each time you add a strip, start sewing from the opposite end as the previous strip to help prevent the unit from curving. Press the seam allowances open. Repeat for the remaining groups to make a total of 20 strip sets. Crosscut the strip sets into 120 segments, 1½" wide. Keep the segments from each strip set together.

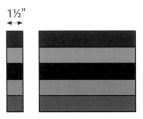

Make 20 strip sets.
Cut 120 segments.

3. Randomly choose five different segments and sew them together along the long edges to make a 25-patch block. Press the seam allowances open. Repeat to make a total of 24 blocks, using as many different combinations as possible.

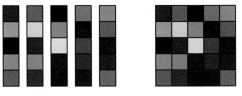

Make 24.

PREPARING FOR APPLIQUÉ

1. Fold the cream 16" square in half vertically, horizontally, and diagonally in both directions and finger-press the folds. Repeat with each of the cream 6" squares. Fold each cream 6" x 36" border strip in half crosswise and lengthwise and finger-press the fold. Use a water-soluble marker or the marking tool of your choice to mark over all of the fold lines. On each border strip, draw another line 1¼" from and parallel to one long edge.

2. Refer to "Making a Master Pattern" (page 6) to make a master pattern for the center square using the pattern on page 62.

3. Make a master pattern of the small appliquéd block using the pattern on page 61.

4. Refer to "Making the Appliqués" (page 6) to trace all of the appliqué shapes for the center square, small appliquéd block, and border, except for the stems, onto freezer paper. Roughly cut out the shapes, and then iron the freezer-paper shapes onto your chosen colors of wool. You'll need 20 sets of appliqués for the small appliquéd blocks, with each set containing four leaves cut from the same wool fabric. Refer to the photo on page 58 and the materials list for fabric choices as needed. Cut out the wool shapes.

5. Refer to "Preassembling Units" (page 7) to assemble the scalloped-flower shapes into units.

ADDING THE APPLIQUÉS

1. Lay the master pattern for the center square on a light box or other light source, and then position the prepared background fabric on top of the master pattern, aligning the reference lines on the pattern and fabric. Pin the background to the master pattern.

2. Refer to "Appliquéing Wool to the Background" (page 7) to glue and staple the prepared appliqué pieces in place, using the burgundy-wool ⅜" x 5" rectangles for the tulip stems and eight burgundy-wool ⅜" x 3" rectangles for the side stems. Work from the bottom layer to the top when placing the appliqués.

3. Using your thread and needle of choice, appliqué the pieces in place with a blanket stitch. Remove the staples.

4. Trim the center square to 15½" x 15½", keeping the design centered.

5. Repeat steps 1–3 with the master pattern for the small appliquéd blocks and each of the

background squares using four matching leaves for each block. Trim each block to 5½" x 5½", keeping the design centered.

6. Refer to the border appliqué placement guide on page 63 to place the remaining appliqués on the border strips. Use the burgundy ⅜" x 2½" rectangles and remaining ⅜" x 3" rectangles for the flower stems and the burgundy ⅜" x 32" strips for the long horizontal stem. Trim each border to 5½" x 35½", keeping the design centered.

ASSEMBLING THE QUILT TOP

1. Refer to the quilt assembly diagram (page 60) to arrange 20 Checkerboard blocks, the small appliquéd blocks, and the appliquéd center block into rows, alternating the Checkerboard and small appliquéd blocks in each row and from row to row.

2. Join the six blocks on each side of the center appliquéd block into three horizontal rows of two blocks each. Join the rows on each side of the center block to make two sections. Press the seam allowances in one direction. Join the sections to the sides of the center block. Press the seam allowances toward the center block.

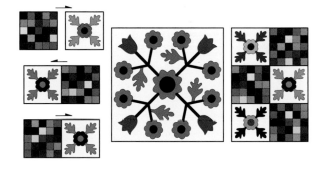

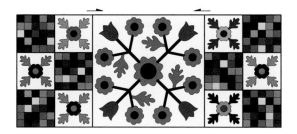

3. Sew the blocks in the remaining rows together. Press the seam allowances toward the small appliquéd blocks. Sew the rows together. Press the seam allowances in one direction.

4. Sew the joined rows from steps 2 and 3 together. Press the seam allowances in one direction.

5. Sew a border strip to each side of the quilt top. Press the seam allowances toward the quilt center. Add the remaining Checkerboard blocks to the ends of the remaining two border strips. Press the seam allowances toward the blocks. Join these borders to the top and bottom of the quilt top. Press the seam allowances toward the quilt center.

FINISHING

1. Cut and piece the backing so it's 4" larger than the quilt top on each side. Sandwich the batting between the backing and quilt top, and baste the layers together.

2. Quilt as desired. I machine quilted an allover design.

3. Trim the backing and batting even with the quilt top. Refer to "Binding" (page 11) to bind the quilt edges with the burgundy-print 2½"-wide strips.

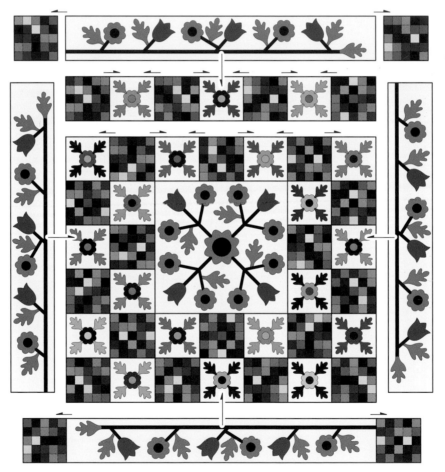

Quilt assembly

Small Block Appliqué Patterns

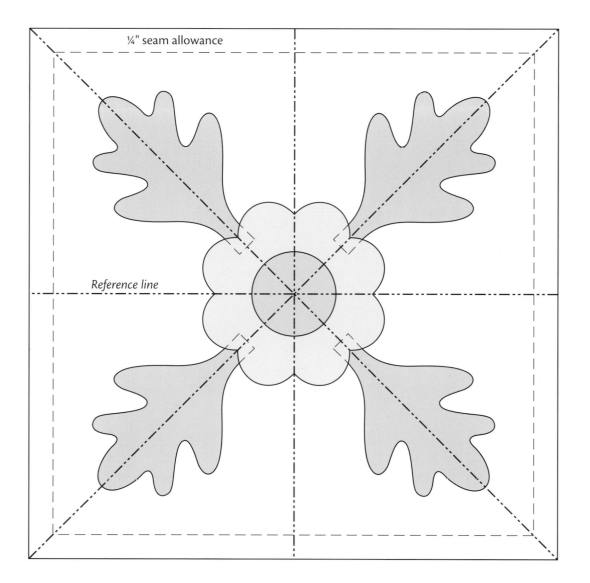

¼" seam allowance

Reference line

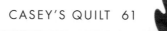

Center Block Appliqué Patterns

Make four quarter patterns.
Join quarter patterns
to make complete pattern.

Reference line

Border Appliqué Patterns

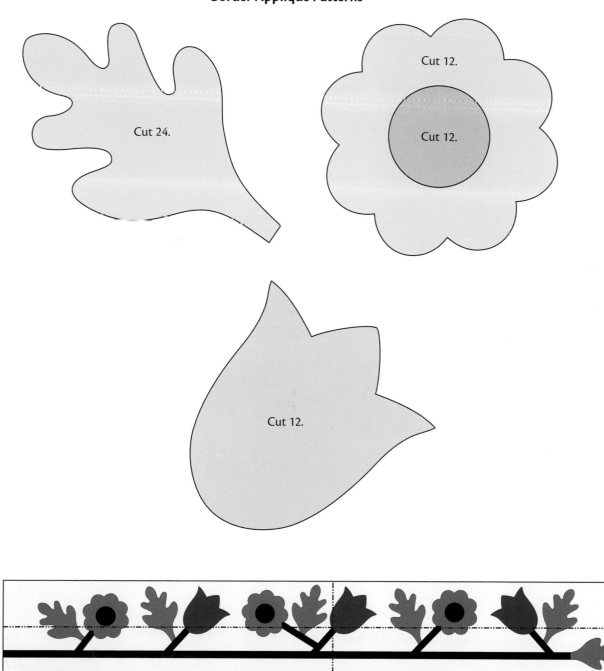

Cut 24.

Cut 12.

Cut 12.

Cut 12.

Border appliqué placement guide

Jeanette's Quilt

I've combined features of two of my all-time favorite blocks into one, with the points of a Bear Paw block surrounding a simplified Album block. Stitching the blocks into vertical rows and adding a curving appliquéd vine and flowers between the rows creates a vivid reflection of my sister Jeanette's vivacity and flair.

– Deirdre

Designed, machine pieced, hand appliquéd, and machine quilted by Deirdre Bond-Abel

Finished Quilt: 72½" x 76½"

MATERIALS

Cotton Fabric

Yardage is based on 42"-wide fabric.

⅓ yard *each* of 20 assorted prints for blocks

2½ yards of cream print for appliquéd-strip backgrounds

2⅓ yards of dark-cream print for block backgrounds

⅔ yard of red print for binding

5 yards of fabric for backing

Felted Wool Fabric

Yardage is based on 48"-wide fabric.

8" x 48" piece of lime-green solid for vine

8" x 48" piece of lime-green houndstooth for leaves and base of yellow flowers

8" x 24" piece of lime-green herringbone for leaves and base of rust-and-teal flowers

8" x 36" piece of yellow for flowers

8" x 36" piece of cherry red for flowers

8" x 36" piece of rust for flowers

8" x 20" piece of teal for flowers

Additional Materials

80" x 84" piece of batting

36"-long piece of freezer paper

Water-soluble glue stick

Stapler

Embroidery floss or flower thread in colors to match wool fabrics

CUTTING

From *each* of the 20 assorted prints, cut:
3 strips, 2½" x 42" (60 total)

From the dark-cream print, cut:
5 strips, 6½" x 42"; crosscut into:

    36 rectangles, 3½" x 6½"

    12 rectangles, 5½" x 6½"

4 strips, 5½" x 42"; crosscut into:

    24 rectangles, 3½" x 5½"

    24 rectangles, 2½" x 5½"

6 strips, 3½" x 42"; crosscut into:

    12 squares, 3½" x 3½"

    72 rectangles, 2½" x 3½"

From the *lengthwise grain* of the cream print, cut:
2 strips, 14½" x 78"

From the lime-green-solid wool, cut:
1 square, 8" x 8"; crosscut into 16 strips, ⅜" x 8"

1 rectangle, 8" x 12"; crosscut into 16 strips, ⅜" x 12"

1 rectangle, 8" x 10½"; crosscut into 16 strips, ⅜" x 10½"

From the red print, cut:
8 strips, 2½" x 42"

Creating a Scrappy Look

There are 15 blocks in this quilt and each block requires four prints. To give the quilt a scrappy look, and also to use the fabric quantities evenly, the prints are used in a different position of the block each time. There will always be a couple of fabrics that will become "good friends," and you'll want to put them together each time; however, the idea of scrappy quilts is to put more unlikely fabric combinations together. This will allow each of the three rows of blocks to look very different.

The bottom of each block "shares" the background pieces of the next block (see the block diagram on page 68), so it's a good idea to pick the four fabrics for each of the five blocks in the row before you start sewing. You'll then need to decide where to place the fabrics in each block.

MAKING THE PIECED-BLOCK ROWS

You'll be making the center row of each block first, and then making the connector units that complete the blocks. Each block is made up of four assorted prints. Refer to the diagram for fabric placement, making sure you don't use the same fabric in the same position more than once.

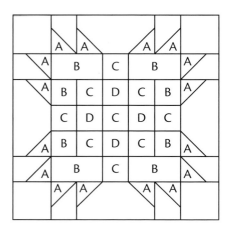

1. Determine which four assorted prints you'll use to make each block in the row, and crosscut the following pieces from the 2½" x 42" strips for *each* block. Refer to the diagram below left for fabric placement. Keep the pieces for each block together.

   Print A: 16 squares, 2½" x 2½"

   Print B: 4 rectangles, 2½" x 4½", and 4 squares, 2½" x 2½"

   Print C: 8 squares, 2½" x 2½"

   Print D: 4 squares, 2½" x 2½"

2. Using the pieces for the first block, refer to "Quick Corner Triangles" (page 10) to draw a diagonal line from corner to corner on the wrong side of each A square. Place a marked square on one end of a dark-cream 2½" x 3½" rectangle as shown. Sew on the marked line. Trim ¼" from the stitching line. Press the triangle toward the corner. Repeat to make a total of two units. Make two additional units, angling the marked line in the opposite direction as shown.

Make 2.

Make 2.

3. Refer to "Quick Corner Triangles" to place two marked A squares on opposite ends of a dark-cream 3½" x 6½" rectangle as shown. Sew, trim, and press as before. Repeat to make a total of two units.

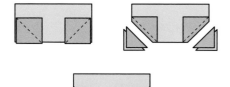

Make 2.

4. Sew a unit from step 2 to each short side of a unit from step 3. Press the seam allowances toward the units from step 2. Repeat to make a total of two side units.

Make 2.

5. Set the remaining A squares aside and label them for block 1. You'll use these later to make the connector units.

6. Arrange the remaining B, C, and D squares and rectangles into five horizontal rows as shown for the block center. Sew the pieces in each row together. Press the seam allowances as indicated. Sew the rows together. Press the seam allowances toward the middle row.

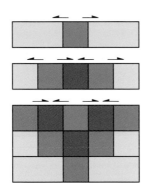

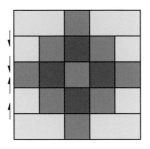

7. Sew the side units to the center unit. Press the seam allowances toward the center unit.

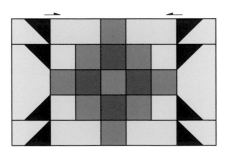

8. Repeat steps 2–7 to make the center rows for the remaining four blocks in the row.

9. To make the connector unit between blocks 1 and 2, refer to "Quick Corner Triangles" to sew four of the remaining marked A squares from each block to two dark-cream 2½" x 5½" rectangles and a cream 5½" x 6½" rectangle as shown.

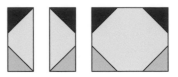

10. Join the units from step 9 and two dark-cream 3½" x 5½" rectangles as shown. Press the seam allowances toward the dark-cream rectangles.

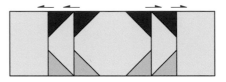

11. Sew the connector unit between the center units of blocks 1 and 2, making sure the A triangles match the appropriate block.

12. Repeat steps 9 and 10 to make the connector units between each block and join the blocks into a row.

13. To make the top row of block 1, refer to "Quick Corner Triangles" to sew the remaining marked A squares to two dark-cream 2½" x 3½" rectangles and a dark-cream 3½" x 6½" rectangle as shown.

14. Join the units from step 13 and two dark-cream 3½" squares as shown. Press the seam allowances toward the squares. Sew the row to the top of block 1. Press the seam allowances toward the block center.

15. Repeat steps 13 and 14 with the remaining A squares from block 5. Sew the row to the bottom of block 5 to complete the block row.

16. Repeat steps 1–15 to make a total of three block rows.

PREPARING AND MAKING THE APPLIQUÉD ROWS

1. Fold each cream 14½" x 78" strip in half lengthwise and finger-press the folds. Use a water-soluble marker or the marking tool of your choice to mark over the lines. These will be your guidelines for placing the appliqué pieces.

2. Refer to "Making a Master Pattern" (page 6) to make a master pattern for the appliquéd row. You'll need to trace the top section, the middle repeat section, and the bottom section onto separate sheets of paper. Be sure to transfer the vertical reference line.

3. Refer to "Making the Appliqués" (page 6) to trace all of the appliqué shapes onto freezer paper, except for the stems. You'll need 16 of *each* flower, 16 leaves, 16 tulip bases, 16 fan-flower bases, and two sets of bottom leaves. Roughly cut out the freezer-paper shapes, and then iron them onto your chosen colors of wool. Refer to the photo on page 66 and the materials list for fabric choices as needed. Cut out the wool shapes.

4. Refer to "Preassembling Units" (page 7) to assemble the tulip and scalloped-flower shapes into units.

5. Lay the master pattern for the top section on a light box or other light source. With the reference lines on the pattern and fabric aligned, position a prepared background strip on top of the master pattern, leaving approximately 2½" of fabric extending above the top of the pattern. Pin the background to the master pattern.

6. Refer to "Appliquéing Wool to the Background" (page 7) to glue and staple your prepared appliqué pieces in place, using the green-solid strips for the stems. Work from the bottom layer to the top when placing the appliqués. When you're done with the top section, lay the repeat section on the light box and realign the background strip. Add the appliqués, and then move the fabric to repeat this section six more times. Finally, use the master pattern for the bottom section to add the bottom leaves.

7. Using your thread and needle of choice, appliqué the pieces in place with a blanket stitch. Remove the staples.

8. Repeat steps 5–7 for the remaining background strip, flipping the patterns over and tracing the design through to the blank side to make a mirror image of the first strip.

9. Trim each appliquéd panel to 12½" x 76½". The easiest way to do this is to place the 6¼" line of your ruler on the centerline of the strip and trim off the excess down one side. Turn the fabric around and trim off the other side in the same manner. Then measure the length and trim to fit the same length as your block rows.

ASSEMBLING AND FINISHING

1. Alternately sew the rows together, positioning the appliquéd rows so the top flower turns toward the quilt center. Press the seam allowances toward the appliquéd rows.

2. Cut and piece the backing so it's 4" larger than the quilt top on each side. Sandwich the batting between the backing and quilt top, and baste the layers together.

3. Quilt as desired. I machine quilted an allover design.

4. Trim the backing and batting even with the quilt top. Refer to "Binding" (page 11) to bind the quilt edges with the red 2½"-wide strips.

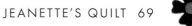

Top section

Reference line

Align with pattern on page 71.

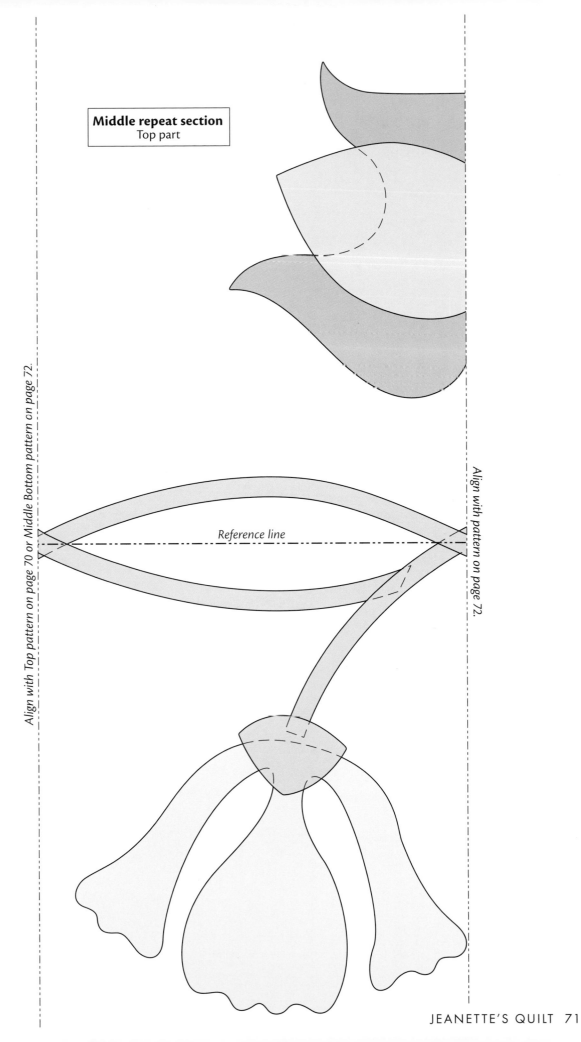

Middle repeat section
Top part

Align with Top pattern on page 70 or Middle Bottom pattern on page 72.

Align with pattern on page 72.

Reference line

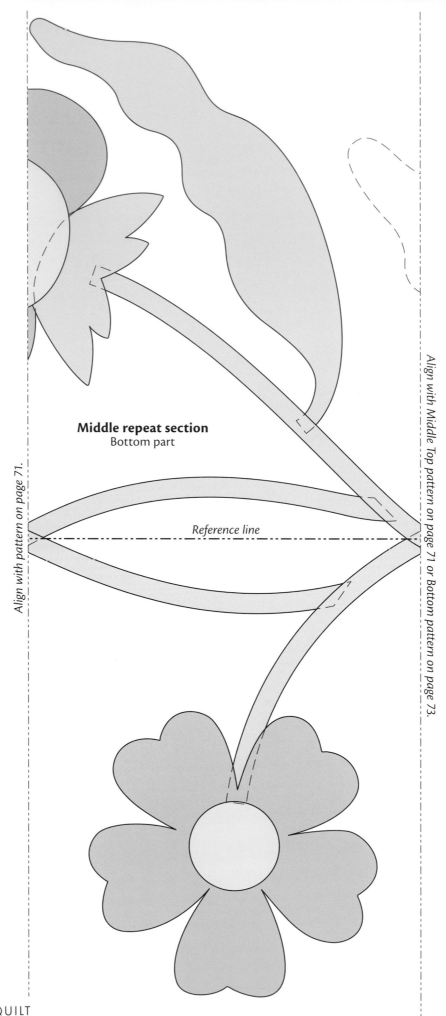

Middle repeat section
Bottom part

Align with pattern on page 71.

Reference line

Align with Middle Top pattern on page 71 or Bottom pattern on page 73.

Bottom section

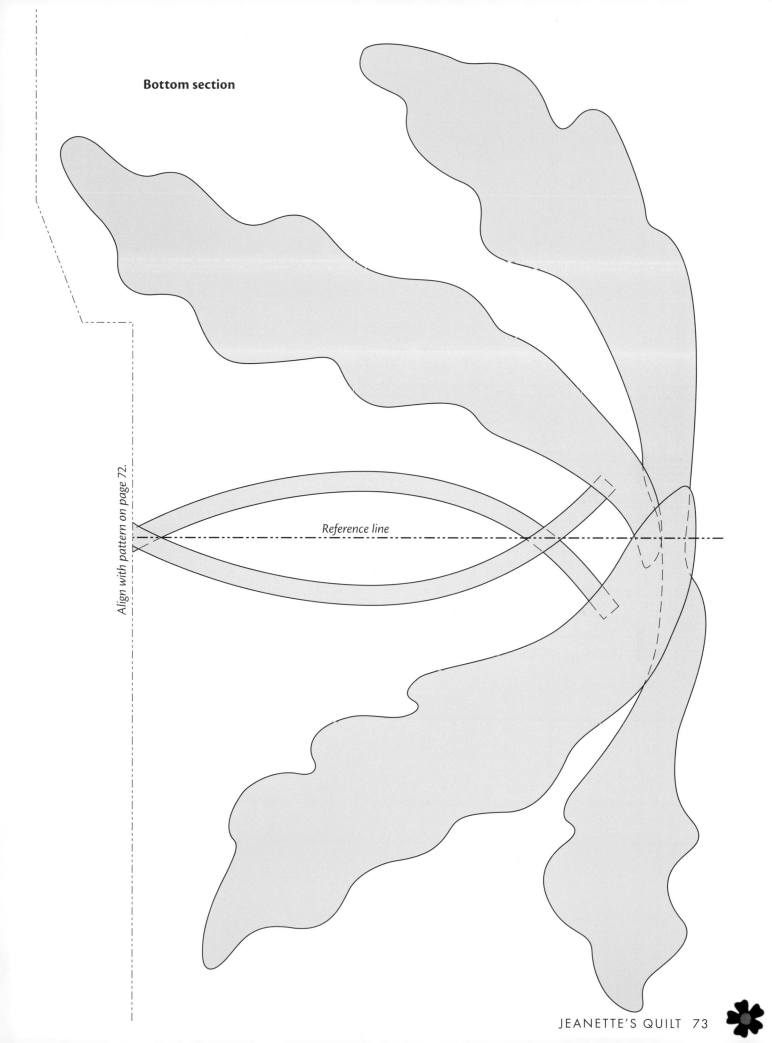

Align with pattern on page 72.

Reference line

One of my favorite blocks is Jacob's Ladder. Here, I've used a variation of the block, set my variation on point, and separated the pieced blocks with wide appliquéd sashing that zigzags around the quilt top. The style of the appliqué is suggestive of the Art Deco period, which reminds me of my grandmother Isabel, whose house was built in that style. I have many happy memories of my stays at Nana's house, and credit her with inspiring my love of needlework.

— Deirdre

Designed, machine pieced, hand appliquéd, and machine quilted by Deirdre Bond-Abel

Finished Quilt: 68⅜" x 68⅜"

MATERIALS

Cotton Fabric

Yardage is based on 42"-wide fabric.

¼ yard *each* of 8 assorted light prints and 8 assorted dark prints for pieced-block half-square-triangle units

⅛ yard *each* of 8 assorted light prints and 8 assorted dark prints for pieced-block four-patch units

1⅝ yards of tan print for side and corner setting triangles

1½ yards of cream print for sashing

⅔ yard of brown print for binding

4⅔ yards of fabric for backing

Felted Wool Fabric

Yardage is based on 48"-wide fabric.

10" x 24" piece of brown for stems

2 yards *total* of assorted colors to match cotton fabrics for flowers and leaves*

*To achieve a nice, scrappy look, I recommend using a variety of colors and textures of wool. I found that 6" x 6" pieces are a good size to work with.

Additional Materials

76" x 76" piece of batting

36"-long piece of freezer paper

Water-soluble glue stick

Stapler

Embroidery floss or flower thread in colors to match wool fabrics

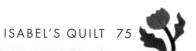

CUTTING

From *each* of the 8 assorted dark and 8 assorted light ¼-yard pieces, cut:

4 squares, 4⅞" x 4⅞" (64 total)

From *each* of the 8 assorted dark and 8 assorted light ⅛-yard pieces, cut:

1 strip, 2½" x 42" (16 total)

From the cream print, cut:

5 strips, 9½" x 42"; crosscut into 10 strips, 9½" x 17½"

From the tan print, cut:

2 squares, 25" x 25"; cut each square into quarters diagonally to yield 8 side setting triangles

2 squares, 13" x 13"; cut each square in half diagonally to yield 4 corner setting triangles

From the brown wool, cut:

10 strips, ⅜" x 24"

8 strips, ⅜" x 9"

16 strips, ⅜" x 9½"

16 strips, ⅜" x 13½"

8 strips, ⅜" x 6"

From the brown print, cut:

8 strips, 2½" x 42"

MAKING THE PIECED BLOCKS

Each of the eight pieced blocks uses four light and four dark 4⅞" squares for the half-square-triangle units and one light and one dark 2½"-wide strip for the four-patch units. Choose eight sets of four fabrics that will give you good contrast for each block.

Six of the blocks are pieced all at once but the two blocks in the center are made in two halves. They'll be joined when the quilt top is sewn into diagonal rows. You may want to decide now which fabrics you're going to place in the center and piece those blocks first.

1. Using one set of four fabrics, refer to "Half-Square-Triangle Units" (page 11) to match each light square with a dark square and make eight half-square-triangle units.

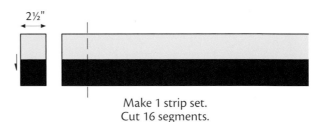

Make 8.

2. Join the light and dark strips along the long edges to make a strip set. Press the seam allowances toward the dark strip. Crosscut the strip set into 16 segments, 2½" wide.

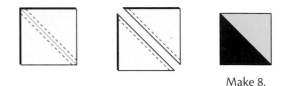

Make 1 strip set.
Cut 16 segments.

3. Join two segments from step 2 as shown to make a four-patch unit. Repeat to make a total of eight units.

Make 8.

4. Arrange the units into four horizontal rows of two half-square-triangle units and two four-patch units each, alternating the units in each row and from row to row. Sew the units in each row together

and press the seam allowances toward the four-patch units.

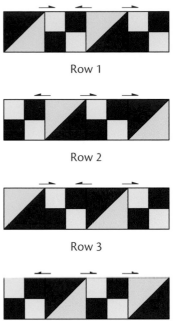

Row 1

Row 2

Row 3

Row 4

5. Sew rows 1 and 2 together and rows 3 and 4 together. Press the seam allowances toward rows 2 and 4. If this will be one of the two center blocks, leave the two halves separated. Otherwise, sew the two halves together to complete the block. Press the seam allowances toward row 3.

Half blocks

Completed block

PREPARING FOR APPLIQUÉ

1. Fold each cream 9½" x 17½" sashing strip in half vertically and horizontally and finger-press the folds. Use a water-soluble marker or the marking tool of your choice to mark over the fold lines.

2. Fold each cream side setting triangle in half along the long edge and finger-press the fold. Mark over the fold lines with the marking tool of your choice. Draw another line ½" from and parallel to both short sides of each triangle.

3. Fold each corner setting triangle in half along the long edge and finger-press the fold. Mark over the fold line with the marking tool of your choice. Draw another line ½" from the long edge of each triangle.

4. Refer to "Making a Master Pattern" (page 6) to make a master pattern of the sashing strip using the pattern on page 79.

5. Make a master pattern of the side setting triangle using the patterns on pages 80 and 81.

6. Make a master pattern of the corner setting triangle using the pattern on page 81.

7. Refer to "Making the Appliqués" (page 6) to trace all of the appliqué shapes for the sashing strips and setting triangles, except for the stems, onto freezer paper. You'll need 10 sets of sashing pieces, eight sets of side setting triangle pieces, and four sets of corner setting triangle pieces. Roughly cut out the freezer-paper shapes, and then iron them onto your chosen colors of wool. Refer to the photo on page 76 and the materials list for fabric choices as needed. Cut out the wool shapes.

8. Refer to "Preassembling Units" (page 7) to assemble the lotus-flower appliqué shapes into units.

ADDING THE APPLIQUÉS

1. Lay the master pattern for the sashing on a light box or other light source, and then position one of the prepared background strips on top of the master pattern, aligning the reference lines on the pattern and fabric. Pin the background to the master pattern.

2. Refer to "Appliquéing Wool to the Background" (page 7) to glue and staple your prepared appliqué pieces in place, using the brown ⅜" x 24" strips for the stems. Work from the bottom layer to the top when placing the appliqués.

3. Using your thread and needle of choice, appliqué the pieces in place with a blanket stitch. Remove the staples.

4. Repeat steps 1–3 with the remaining sashing strips to make five sashing strips and five mirror-image sashing strips.

5. Trim the sashing strips to 8½" x 16½", keeping the design centered.

6. Repeat steps 1–3 with the master pattern for the side setting triangles and each of the side setting fabric triangles. Trim ¼" off the short edges, but leave the long edges untrimmed until the quilt top is sewn together.

7. Repeat steps 1–3 with the master pattern for the corner setting triangles and the corner setting fabric triangles. Trim ¼" off the long edge, but leave the short edges untrimmed until the quilt top is sewn together.

ASSEMBLING THE QUILT TOP

1. Refer to the diagram below to arrange the blocks, half blocks, sashing strips, and setting triangles into five diagonal rows. Rearrange the blocks as needed so that you have a good distribution of colors. Make sure the sashing strips are positioned so that the vines curve correctly. Sew the pieces in each row together, adding the corner triangles to rows 1 and 5 last. Press the seam allowances toward the pieced blocks.

2. Sew the rows together. Press the seam allowances in one direction.

FINISHING

1. Cut and piece the backing fabric so it's 4" larger than the quilt top on each side. Sandwich the batting between the backing and quilt top, and baste the layers together.

2. Quilt as desired. I used an allover design to stitch my quilt.

3. Trim the backing and batting even with the quilt top. Refer to "Binding" (page 11) to bind the quilt edges with the brown 2½"-wide strips.

Sashing Appliqué Patterns

Make two patterns. Rotate one pattern 180°
and join patterns to make complete pattern.

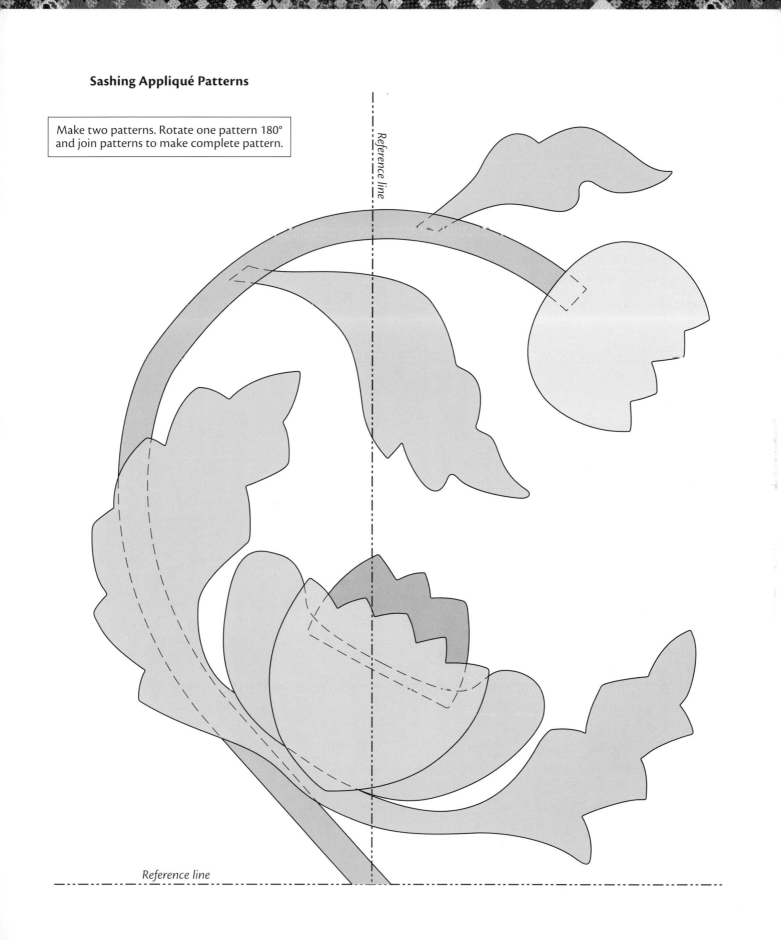

Reference line

Reference line

Side Setting Triangle Appliqué Patterns

Align patterns as indicated to make half pattern. Make two patterns. Flip one pattern over and trace design to blank side to make mirror image. Join original half pattern and mirror-image half pattern to make complete pattern.

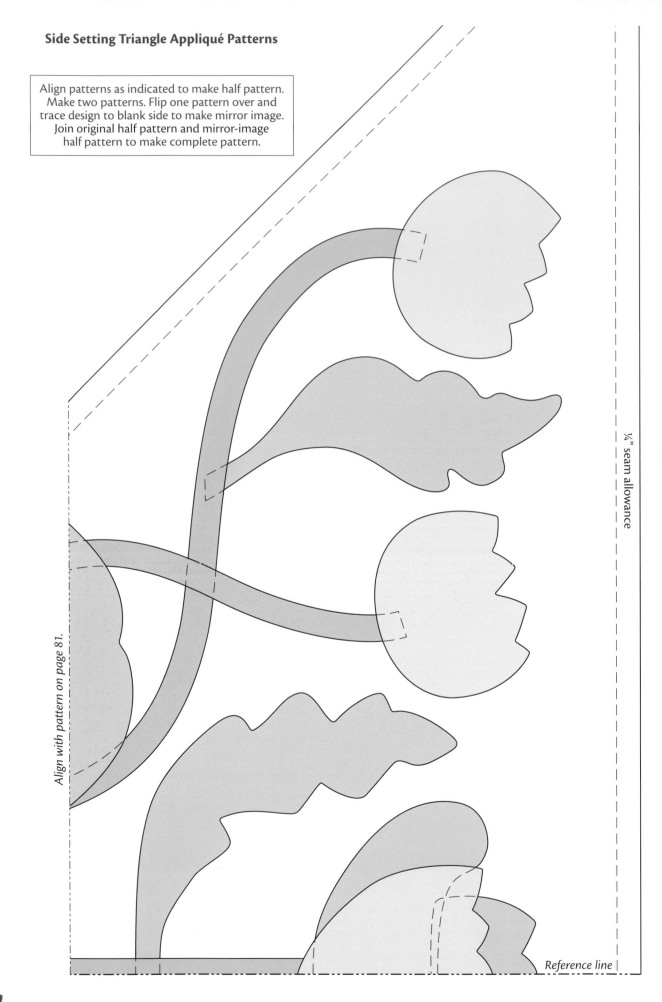

¼" seam allowance

Align with pattern on page 81.

Reference line

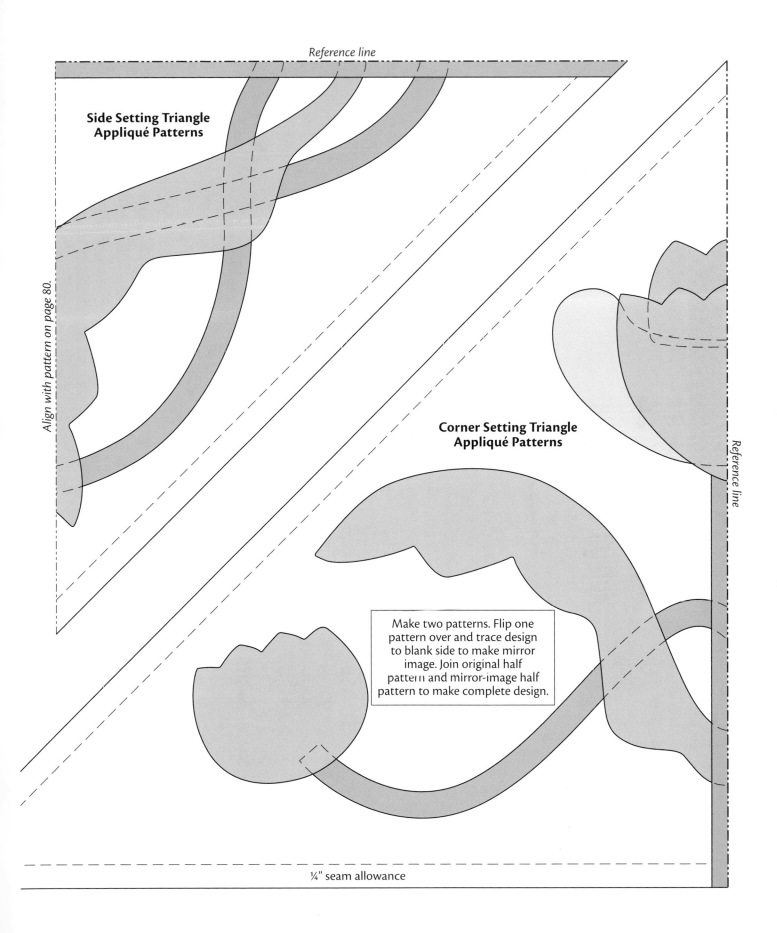

**Side Setting Triangle
Appliqué Patterns**

Align with pattern on page 80.

**Corner Setting Triangle
Appliqué Patterns**

Make two patterns. Flip one
pattern over and trace design
to blank side to make mirror
image. Join original half
pattern and mirror-image half
pattern to make complete design.

Reference line

¼" seam allowance

Working with beautiful felted wool and reproduction fabrics doesn't have to be limited to quilts. You can incorporate these fabrics into your everyday wardrobe with this beautiful scarf. The appliqué detail on the scarf features felted wool along with some added texture and dimension using cotton fabric and reverse appliqué. One side of the scarf has a long design on it, and the other half has a shorter version, for asymmetrical beauty. This scarf is named "Sophia" after the gorgeous line of reproduction fabric.

— Deirdre

Designed, hand appliquéd, and machine pieced by Deirdre Bond-Abel
Finished Scarf: 8½" x 95"

MATERIALS

Cotton Fabric

Yardage is based on 42"-wide fabric.

1 yard of red print for lining

¼ yard of red print for leaf reverse-appliqué insert

Felted Wool Fabric

Yardage is based on 48"-wide fabric.

⅝ yard of black for scarf background

5" x 24" piece of cherry red for outer large flowers, outer bud, and stems

10" x 10" square of dark red for scalloped top of large flowers, inner bud, and leaves

10" x 10" square of brownish red for inner large flowers, flower bases, and leaves

Additional Materials

18"-long piece of freezer paper

Water-soluble glue stick

Stapler

Embroidery floss or flower thread in colors to match wool fabrics

CUTTING

From the black wool, cut:

2 strips, 9" x 48"

From the red print for reverse-appliqué insert, cut:

1 rectangle, 6½" x 13"

1 rectangle, 6½" x 5"

From the cherry-red wool, cut:

1 strip, ⅜" x 22"*

1 strip, ⅜" x 13"*

I do not cut my stem strips on the bias and find that they still curve nicely.

From the red print for lining, cut:

3 strips, 9" x 42"

PREPARING THE BACKGROUND FOR APPLIQUÉ

1. Using a white marking pen or pencil, draw a line through the lengthwise center of both black strips.

2. Refer to "Making a Master Pattern" (page 6) to make a master pattern of the large motif using the patterns on pages 86 and 87. This master pattern will also be used for the smaller motif on the opposite end of the scarf, so be sure to transfer the dashed lines for that flower to the pattern.

3. Refer to "Making the Appliqués" (page 6) to trace all of the appliqué shapes, except for the stems but including the reverse-appliqué leaves, onto freezer paper. You'll need two large flowers, one bud, one bud leaf, and two of each of the remaining leaves. Roughly cut out the freezer-paper shapes. Set aside the shapes for the cutout leaves. Iron the remaining freezer-paper shapes onto your chosen colors of wool. Refer to the photo on page 82 and the materials list for fabric choices as needed. Cut out the wool shapes.

4. Refer to "Preassembling Units" (page 7) to assemble the large flower and bud pieces into units.

5. Cut out the freezer-paper shapes for the reverse-appliqué leaves on the drawn lines.

6. Refer to "Appliquéing Wool to the Background" (page 7) to glue and staple your prepared appliqué pieces in place, using the cherry-red ⅜"-wide strips for the stems. Because you're working with a dark background fabric, use the marked reference line to help you place the appliqués for the large motif on one end of a black strip and the appliqués for the smaller motif on one end of the remaining black strip. The bottom leaves should be placed approximately 3" from the short end of each strip. Position all of the leaves first, using the freezer-paper shape for the cutout leaves. Once you're happy with the position of the leaves, iron the freezer-paper leaves in place and glue and staple the wool leaves in place.

Paper-Template Guide

If you're not comfortable eyeballing the placement of your design, you can make a paper template to guide you. Use your master pattern to trace the left-hand reference line and the center reference line. Add the curve of the stem and the outline of the two reverse-appliqué leaves on the left side of the pattern. Cut along the left edge of the curved stem line, and then cut around the outline of the two leaves. You'll have a pattern with a straight edge on the left side and a curved edge on the right side with two leaf shapes cut into the middle.

7. Trace around the freezer-paper leaves with a white marking pen or pencil. Cut out the shapes on the marked line. Refer to "Reverse Appliqué" (page 9) to reverse appliqué the leaves using the red-print rectangles. Use the larger red piece to cover both leaves of the larger motif and the smaller rectangle for the small motif.

8. Position the remaining appliqués in place, working from the bottom layer to the top. Use the cherry-red wool strips for the stems.

9. Using the thread and needle of your choice, appliqué the pieces in place with a blanket stitch. Remove the staples.

COMPLETING THE SCARF

1. With right sides together, sew the two black strips together at the short non-appliquéd ends. Press the seam allowances open.

2. Sew the three red 9" x 42" lining strips together end to end to make one long strip. Press the seam allowances open.

3. Measure the length of the black strip from step 1. Cut the lining strip to the length measured.

4. Pin the wool and lining strips right sides together. Stitch the strips together along all of the edges, leaving a 6" opening on one side for turning. Turn the scarf right side out through the opening and press all the edges and corners well. Hand slip-stitch the opening closed.

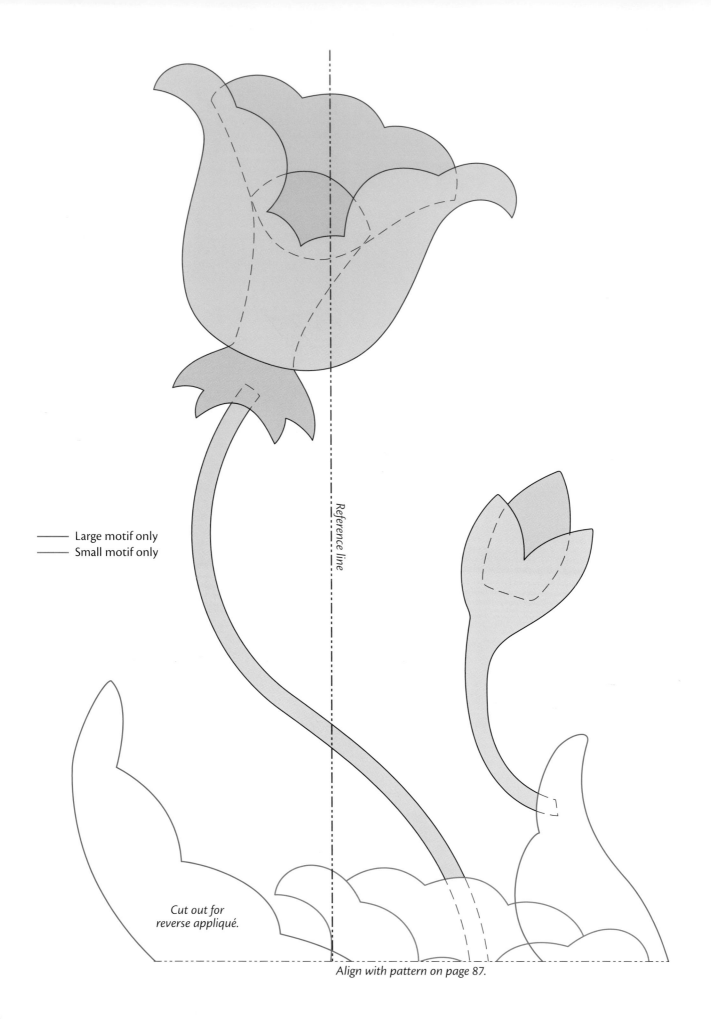

Large motif only
Small motif only

Reference line

Cut out for
reverse appliqué.

Align with pattern on page 87.

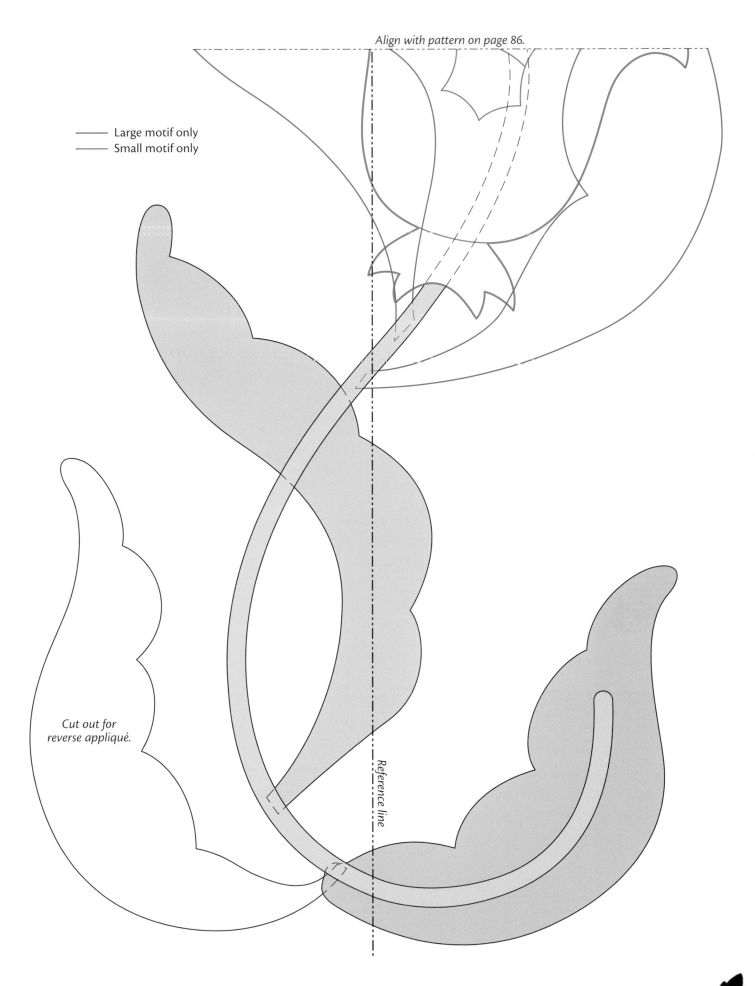

Align with pattern on page 86.

——— Large motif only
——— Small motif only

Cut out for
reverse appliqué.

Reference line

MATERIALS

Cotton Fabric

Yardage is based on 42"-wide fabric.

¾ yard of cream print for background

3" x 13" strip *each* of 3 assorted blue prints for large Nine Patch blocks

2" x 18" strip of brown print for small Nine Patch blocks and flower reverse-appliqué inserts

2" x 8" strip *each* of 3 assorted brown prints for small Nine Patch blocks

½ yard of brown print for binding

⅔ yard of fabric for backing

Felted Wool Fabric

Yardage is based on 48"-wide fabric.

12" x 12" square of mushroom for leaves

3" x 16" strip of brown for stems

6" x 12" rectangle of teal for flowers

Additional Materials

18"-long piece of freezer paper

Water-soluble glue stick

Stapler

Embroidery floss or flower thread in colors to match wool fabrics

Simple Nine Patch blocks combine with appliqué in strong masculine colors to add warmth and style to any guy's room. I made this one for my son, Mitchell, who has a beautiful 1930s home full of wonderful old treasures. Whether used on a fireplace mantel or on a narrow hall table, this small piece is sure to draw attention.

— *Deirdre*

Designed, machine pieced, hand appliquéd, and hand quilted by Deirdre Bond-Abel

Finished Runner: 17" x 31½"

CUTTING

From the 2" x 18" brown strip, cut:
5 squares, 1½" x 1½"

From *each* of the 3 assorted brown prints, cut:
5 squares, 1½" x 1½" (15 total)

From the cream print, cut:
1 strip, 8½" x 32"

2 rectangles, 3½" x 9"

2 squares, 5½" x 5½"; cut each square into quarters diagonally to yield 8 side setting triangles

2 squares, 5⅛" x 5⅛"; cut each square in half diagonally to yield 4 corner setting triangles

12 squares, 2½" x 2½"

16 squares, 1½" x 1½"

From *each* of the 3 assorted blue prints, cut:
5 squares, 2½" x 2½" (15 total)

From the brown wool, cut:
2 strips, ⅜" x 14"

2 strips, ⅜" x 12"

2 strips, ⅜" x 16"

From the *bias* of the brown print for binding, cut:
Enough 2½"-wide strips to make a strip 107" long when joined end to end

MAKING THE BLOCKS

1. Arrange five matching brown 1½" squares and four cream 1½" squares into three horizontal rows. Sew the squares in each row together. Press the seam allowances toward the brown squares. Sew the rows together. Press the seam allowances toward the top and bottom rows. Repeat to make a total of four small Nine Patch blocks.

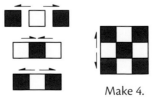

Make 4.

2. Repeat step 1 with the blue and cream 2½" squares to make three large Nine-Patch blocks.

ASSEMBLING THE RUNNER

1. Sew a side setting triangle to adjacent sides of each small Nine Patch block. Press the seam allowances toward the triangles.

Make 4.

2. Refer to the diagram to arrange the units from step 1, the large Nine Patch blocks, and the cream corner triangles into diagonal rows. Sew the units from step 1 and the corner triangles to opposite sides of the large Nine Patch blocks first. Press the seam allowances toward the large Nine Patch blocks. Sew the rows together. Press the seam allowances toward the center Nine Patch block. Add the remaining corner setting triangles. Press the seam allowances toward the triangles.

3. Sew a cream 3½" x 9" rectangle to each end of the pieced strip. Press the seam allowances toward the rectangles. Add the cream 8½" x 32" strip to one long edge of the pieced strip. Press the seam allowance toward the cream strip.

PREPARING FOR APPLIQUÉ

1. Refer to "Making a Master Pattern" (page 6) to make a master pattern of the runner appliqué using the patterns on pages 92–95.

2. Refer to "Making the Appliqués" (page 6) to trace all of the appliqué shapes, except for the stems, onto freezer paper. Roughly cut out the shapes, and then iron the freezer-paper shapes onto your chosen colors of wool. Refer to the photo on page 88 and the materials list for fabric choices as needed. Cut out the wool shapes.

3. Refer to "Reverse Appliqué" (page 9) to reverse appliqué the cutout sections of the large flowers using the leftover fabric from the brown strip.

4. Lay the master pattern on a light box or other light source, and then position the prepared background fabric on top of the master pattern, lining up the seam lines of the pieced section with the pattern reference lines. Pin the background to the master pattern.

5. Refer to "Appliquéing Wool to the Background" (page 7) to glue and staple your prepared appliqué pieces in place, using the brown wool strips for the stems. Work from the bottom layer to the top when placing the appliqués.

6. Using your thread and needle of choice, appliqué the pieces in place using a blanket stitch. Remove the staples.

FINISHING

1. Cut the backing so it's 4" larger than the runner top on each side. Sandwich the batting between the backing and quilt top, and baste the layers together. Use the curve pattern to curve the bottom corners of the runner.

2. Quilt as desired. I hand quilted my runner with a crosshatch pattern.

3. Trim the backing and batting even with the table runner top. Refer to "Binding" (page 11) to bind the runner edges with the brown-print 2½"-wide bias strips.

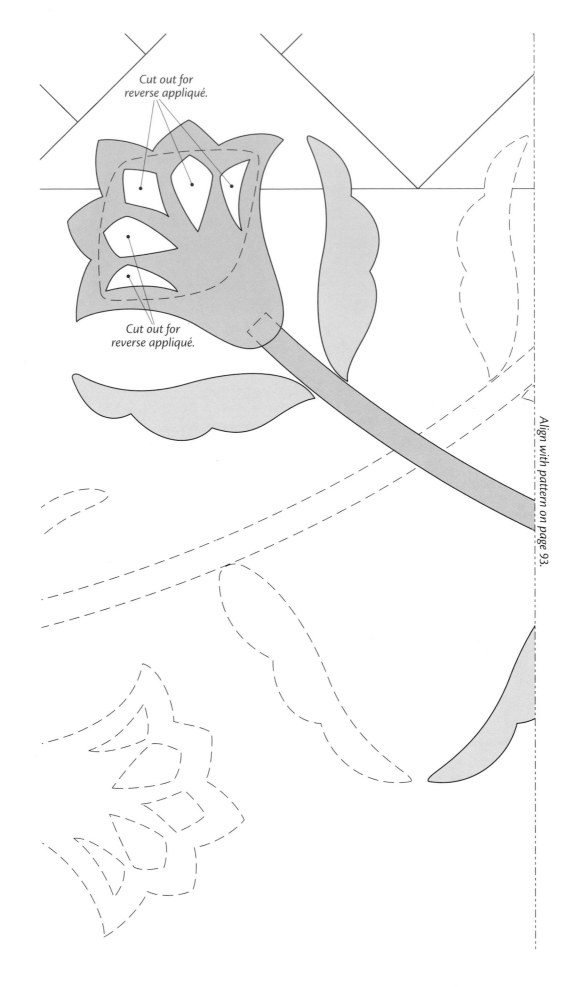

Cut out for
reverse appliqué.

Cut out for
reverse appliqué.

Align with pattern on page 93.

Align with pattern on page 92.

Align with pattern on page 94.

Cut out for
reverse
appliqué.

Cut out for
reverse
appliqué.

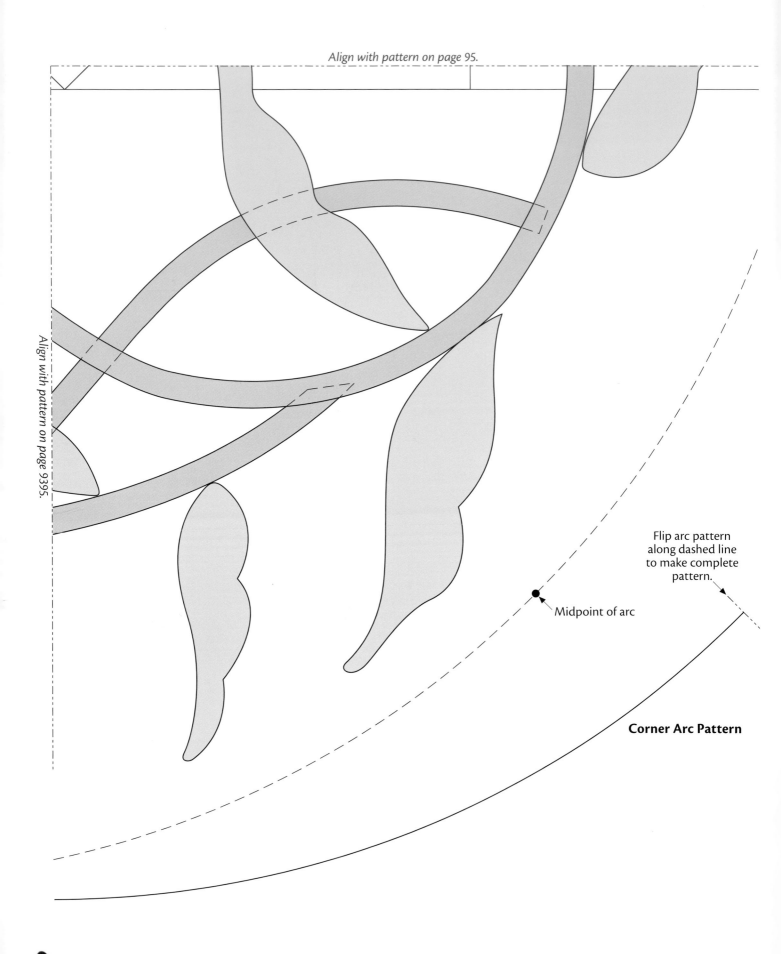

Align with pattern on page 95.

Align with pattern on page 9395.

Flip arc pattern
along dashed line
to make complete
pattern.

● Midpoint of arc

Corner Arc Pattern

Cut out for
reverse appliqué.

Cut out for
reverse appliqué.

Align with pattern on page 94.

About the Authors

Leonie (left) has had a love of sewing for as long as she can remember. Her first attempt at quilting was just after her eldest daughter was born 16 years ago, and from then on she has never looked back. Most of what she does she has taught herself along the way through trial and error, reading books, and attending classes here and there. One of her dreams was to one day have her own quilt shop— a dream that she realized six years ago. She shares the quilt shop, The Quilted Crow, with her best friend, Deirdre, "the other crow." Leonie is married and has two beautiful daughters. She lives in Hobart, Tasmania, Australia.

Deirdre (right) is married and the mother to two beautiful children. In her former life she was a nurse who dreamed of being a quilt-shop owner. She has been designing her own quilts to keep and to teach quilting for about 20 years. Six years ago she joined forces with her best friend, Leonie, to become one half of The Quilted Crow. Her family, animals, quilting, antiques, and music are her passions. What she loves most is sharing her love of wool appliqué with other like-minded people. Visit The Quilted Crow at www.thequiltedcrow.com.au.